D1374194

THE STARFISH FILES

One Leader's Account of
Insight & Inspiration
Under Duress

Alex Hiam

INSIGHTS for Training & Development

HRD Press, Inc. • Amherst • Massachusetts

The Starfish Files

Copyright © 2005 by Alex Hiam

Published by: HRD Press, Inc.
                 22 Amherst Road
                 Amherst, MA 01002
                 800-822-2801 (U.S. and Canada)
                 413-253-3488
                 413-253-3490 (fax)
                 http://www.hrdpress.com

                 INSIGHTS for Training & Development
                 98 Spring St.
                 Amherst MA 01002
                 (413) 549-6100
                 www.insightsfortraining.com

ISBN: 0-87425-836-7

Printed in Canada

Table of Contents

Acknowledgments

Thanks to the many associates, customers, and leaders who commented on early drafts of this book: your help and encouragement was invaluable. Special thanks to Mary George for her editorial wizardry, to Elizabeth Finney for bringing the book to life in watercolor and pencil, to Eileen Klockars for designing this edition so ably, to Noelle Hiam for encouraging my storytelling whims, to Stephanie Sousbies for managing the office so well that I actually have *time* to write, to the staff of the U.S. Coast Guard's Leadership Development Center for their early adoption of this book in their curriculum, and, especially, to Bob Carkhuff for helping to bring this book and the entire Strategic Leadership program to life. Every worthwhile project is a team effort, and books are no exception!

Introduction

T his story first came to me in a series of battered files stuffed with handwritten notes. Their author, who chooses to remain anonymous, had wished to share certain rather unusual experiences recorded in those notes, and we have simply converted his files into the chapters that follow.

That much is simple to explain. Far less simple, and perhaps impossible to explain, is the specific nature of the experiences documented in those files. I suspect you will be as skeptical about it as I was. And I admit, even now, it is hard for me to believe that these events indeed happened. Yet the evidence is irrefutable.

But let me begin at the beginning.

Some people go to the beach for relaxation, others for inspiration. I fall into both categories myself—I find that the gentle swish of surf on sand not only calms my nerves but often gives me fresh ideas as well. Beaches are good problem-solvers in our busy, stressful world.

I was not too surprised, then, when an acquaintance of mine sent me some notes on business management after a summer vacation by the sea. The notes arrived in a folder on which was scribbled "The Starfish File," an intriguing label that caught my attention despite my overflowing "in" box.

His cover letter reminded me who he was—at that time, a low-ranking manager with a somewhat unprofitable firm—and explained that the enclosed notes had been inspired by an amazing seaside experience. This material, he thought, might be beneficial to other managers who, like him, were struggling with performance challenges or wondering how to produce improved results. Could I, as a successful author and business professional, take a serious look at this material?

Suddenly his file lost its intrigue.

I had found myself in this position before, obliged to make appropriately polite and supportive noise over some acquaintance's "baby"—a first attempt to write a book. And it was not that I wished to avoid helping a prospective author, or that I hoped to dodge the embarrassment of having to point out, yet again, that it's tough to write a good book, but . . .

I slipped the file into one of the larger piles of paperwork on my desk, and forgot about it. Until the next file arrived.

This time it held only a brief message, one I could not easily dismiss as I had rarely received a more extraordinary piece of correspondence. Here it is, reproduced in full:

URGENT

Re: Starfish File

Do not—*I repeat, do not!*—under any circumstance read or reproduce the file I sent. Instruct you to destroy file without opening. My reputation, perhaps even sanity, at stake. *Destroy at once!*

There are times, fortunately not very often, when a person is forced to look deep into his own soul and see what kind of stuff he's made of. For me, this was one of those times. And what I saw there was composed of a good deal of integrity, but also quite a few parts curiosity.

I knew I had to sneak a peek—a *quick* peek—into that first file before destroying it. Thus I commenced a careful but eager search through my piles of paperwork.

I suppose that, in hindsight, I might have recalled the myth of Pandora's Box, and questioned the wisdom of what I was doing. I might have taken it as fate's warning sign that my search was fruitless. And I certainly might have considered how foolish I'd feel in hindsight as I tore my office apart in frustration. But as they say, hindsight has 20-20 vision, and I definitely do not.

Luckily, I am also composed of a few parts work ethic, which forced me to abandon my search, tidy up, and get back to my ordinary projects and duties. Time passed, carrying off my memory of the whole strange affair.

Then the third message arrived.

This time it came in the dead of night, crackling through a phone line into my voice mail. Although it was difficult to follow, the basics were clear: my acquaintance had just had another unusual experience, even more extraordinary than the first (whatever that was), and had changed his mind about "The Starfish File." In fact, did I still have the file? It was his original and he didn't have a copy.

He also said that he had decided to draft records of his "additional encounters" (whatever that meant), and would I be so kind as to keep the files and help organize them? Then they would be ready for him to share with the general public should that step prove advisable in the future.

Well, I admit that at this point, I highly doubted the sanity of the man. Those doubts seemed confirmed the next day when, through a phone inquiry from my office to his, I learned he had gone off on a business trip without leaving a forwarding address or phone number. I suspected he had in fact checked into a mental institution. As it turned out, he *had* checked in—but not to a hospital. He was staying at a cheap seaside motel, so that he could take a long mid-week walk along the beach.

Ah, the things you can get away with when you're a boss. Even a low-ranking one.

To make a long story short (because it is *his* story that you need to read, not mine), I received several additional files over the course of that summer, with occasional follow-ups later in the year, and in truth, I cannot fault my acquaintance for wondering whether it was advisable to admit to these experiences in public. Yet the insights he had gained, and the undeniable benefit he was reaping from applying those insights, convinced him that he had a duty to share his discoveries with the world, regardless of the personal cost. And when I pointed out that he could remain anonymous, and thus not threaten his rising status in the corporate world, he wholeheartedly agreed to publishing a full record of his experiences.

The rest, as they say, is history. I suppose some may call it fantasy, but then again, there are skeptics in every field, and perhaps more in the field of business than any other. For a struggling young manager to receive valuable guidance from a helpful older mentor—that is not too hard to believe, in and of itself. But that the mentor should be . . . Well, as I say, it is not my story, and I should really let you examine the files and decide for yourself.

Fortunately, the first file did eventually resurface. It was stuck to the underside of a particularly nasty-looking folder that, being from my accountant, went unread until April 14 of the following year. Once that initial piece of the puzzle fell into place, it was a relatively simple matter for me to help my new friend pull his story into order and prepare it for publication.

Will there ever be more Starfish Files?

We really don't know. If there are, I doubt they will come from my friend, who now is associated with the senior executive's office of one of the world's largest and most successful organizations. He himself feels grateful to have been the conduit for the information you are about to enjoy. But he did not choose that role; he was chosen. And so, perhaps someone else with an urgent need will be selected for similar encounters at a place and time that we cannot anticipate. Only one thing is certain: if it does happen, it will happen by the sea.

Our hope is that these marvels will indeed continue, affording us the chance to expand the Starfish Files and deepen our understanding of the principles and practices they convey. For now, though, we feel privileged to offer you this lightly edited but completely authentic account, drawn directly from the files that were sent to me.

If by chance you can guess the identity of the manager behind the files, please respect his privacy and his strong desire to remain in the background. He has a business to run, and there are those hard-nosed sorts, especially among the less imaginative of Wall Street investors, whose rosy reports on his management prowess might swing the other way were the source of his inspiration to become known.

But let me just say this. He is clearly not insane. Whether or not you trust the veracity of his story, the business community and much of the world view him as one of the more level-headed and competent managers practicing today. I do not know if it would be fair to attribute *all* of his success to the events recounted in the Starfish Files, as he is wont to do; but I certainly do know that however outlandish those events may seem, their net results are very real. (No pun intended.)

At the core of my friend's success is his uncanny knack for creating a high-performance work climate in which everyone has star potential and employees truly do accomplish amazing things. And this knack has developed in those who have since emulated his method. Thus its "magic," so it seems, is accessible to everyone.

As for myself, I do not care from whence a soul draws inspiration, as long as the owner of that soul does the right thing when the time comes. With that in mind and without further ado, here are the files themselves, presented to you as they were presented to me, free of annotation or explanation. I'll be interested to see what *your* soul makes of them.

1. Beach Combing

Once upon a time, on a lonely stretch of beach, a burned-out manager sat wearily on a rock. His eyes were downcast under a furrowed brow. His hands were buried deep in his pockets. If he noticed the gentle rumble of the waves on the sand or the happy cries of the gulls on the wind, he didn't show it. His mind, it seemed, was somewhere else—perhaps *under* the rock. And in a sense, it was.

His mind was back in the office where he would ordinarily be. Thinking about work made him terribly unhappy, but he couldn't help himself. Work was a burden he couldn't put down because he was so worried that no one else would take it up.

Sometimes it seemed that he was the only one who saw the big picture, who cared enough to make sure everything went well. He alone, it appeared, put the success of the venture above his own personal needs and wants.

Worst of all, he felt that his people just weren't as committed to the work as he. They often seemed to put more care and intelligence into outside activities. Some were attentive parents; others were active athletes. Still others were avid volunteers, or fanatic collectors, or devoted artists. Some of them seemed to be all of these and more, none of which had a thing to do with work or earned them one red cent! True, sometimes they showed the same initiative and enthusiasm on the job, but not nearly as often as he wished.

The sun burned down on the back of his neck and a drop of perspiration dampened his brow, but the manager didn't notice. He was too busy worrying. "Wouldn't it be nice," he thought, "to come back from my vacation and discover that my employees had taken the initiative to solve a major problem or implement a great new idea while I was gone?"

His employees' attitudes hadn't bothered him as much in previous years, but right now his group was facing some serious challenges. Sales were flat and costs were rising. There was new competition and new technology to master, and many other challenges the manager was not sure how to handle. He sensed they were in for a bumpy ride and worried that he might not come up with all the answers on his own. Yet his people acted as though it was up to *him* to make everything all right. When problems upset their routines, they were more likely to complain or become angry than to come up with solutions.

A sudden noise—*crack!*—interrupted the manager's thoughts. A stubbornly shut clam had fallen out of the sky and bounced off a nearby rock. With a great swoop, a white gull snatched it up, then climbed into the air again, circled, and took careful aim. *Crack!* This time the clam split open, and soon the gull was enjoying its meal. "What an innovative technique!" the manager thought. "I wonder where that bird learned a trick like that. One thing's for sure, it didn't need a manager to tell it what to do."

He returned to his worries, praying that nothing would go wrong while he was on vacation. Two whole workdays without his supervision . . . He hated to think what might happen in an emergency, and he knew that even if nothing serious went wrong, there would be a backlog of approvals and minor problems for him when he got back.

Too bad his cell phone didn't get good reception here at the beach. He hated being out of touch.

He decided that he'd go into the office extra early on Tuesday morning and try to catch up. If he was tired after the long drive home on Monday night, well, it couldn't be helped. Or could it? Was there some way out of this management maze, some easier approach? (He paused to wipe the sweat from his brow.) Was it possible to share the burden, or better yet, to transform this sense of burden into a feeling of opportunity and positive possibilities? If he could only *somehow* get his people to tackle their work with a more positive attitude, a little more initiative, a shared feeling of ownership and personal responsibility for their success . . .

The manager watched the gull finish its meal and then soar into the air again, calling out a joyful self-congratulation.

He wondered what he would have to do differently to create the kind of workplace he wished for. He imagined that some workplaces *were* different, that in some organizations everyone shared the journey equally and gave it their all. How positive and energizing that might be. But it was a hard thing to achieve, as he remembered from bitter personal experience.

Last year he'd heard about a method of challenging employees to be more motivated and positive. Excited, he had brought up the question of attitude at a staff meeting. This kicked off a lively discussion in which many employees agreed that it would be good to have a better workplace. But soon they fell into a debate about why attitudes were negative and who was to blame. He had grown tired of listening to this gripe session, so he pointed out to them that they had the power to choose their own mood. And he challenged each of them to come to work every day in a positive, can-do mood instead of a negative one.

This didn't go over nearly as well as he had hoped. He realized it was like trying to water a desert. Good ideas were overwhelmed by the prevailing attitudes, and soon everyone was complaining that it was impossible to be in a good mood when management did this and customers did that and your associates did the other thing. He felt like he was just wasting his time, and eventually gave up. In hindsight he realized that you don't change people's attitudes by just *telling* them to be different, any more than you cure an illness by telling the patient to feel better. Sure, people can choose what mood they'd *like* to have, but it isn't always easy to change old patterns and achieve the desired state—especially when the workplace routines seem to push everyone back into their old negative patterns. He realized that the attitudes he wanted to change must have deep roots.

Sighing a big sigh, the manager turned his gaze dully toward the sea . . . and suddenly came alert.

Something bright had flashed in the surf. A large fish? Yes, there was the graceful splash of a tail, the glitter of sun on silvery scales. But what would such a big fish be doing so close to shore?

And wait, what in the world was *that?* Something seemed odd about the creature's body. Or was it swimming with a person? He could've sworn he'd seen a woman's head and long rings of wet curls as the creature dove through the crest of a wave.

Puzzled, the manager got up and walked down the beach.

"Hello!" a musical voice rang out. "Would you like to make a wish?"

The manager looked around for the source of the voice, but could see no one else nearby.

"Over here," the voice called. "No, not on the land, in the water!" Before the manager could turn toward the sea again, he heard a splash. Then a jet-spray of saltwater doused him from head to toe. Wiping his eyes to clear his vision and gasping from the shock of the cold spray, he turned around—and was even more shocked to see the head and torso of a graceful woman waving to him from the surf with a large *fishtail* flapping behind her.

"Wha . . . are . . . who . . .?"

"Yes, that's right, over here," she said. "Do you have your wish prepared?"

The manager gaped at her. If he hadn't been so distracted, he might have realized that his expression made him look more like a fish than she did. She had a warm, friendly smile, and pearly teeth under a broad nose. She really looked quite human except for the strange flash of green light in her eyes and the way she let her thick hair float loosely on the water around her. Human from the waist up, at least. But somewhere around the middle of her torso, silver scales began to appear, giving her a most inhuman appearance.

"Are . . . are you . . . a *mermaid?*" the manager asked uncertainly, wondering if his eyes were deceiving him.

"Sea person, yes, and proud of it" she replied, leaping free of the waves and diving back in with a single swish of her tail and a surprising lack of modesty. "Now, about your wish. What is it?"

"You mean you can grant magic wishes?" the manager asked in amazement, stepping closer to the sea so he could hear her more clearly over the surf.

"Well, not magic maybe, but I give awfully good advice. I'm a manager, you see, so my specialty is helping others achieve difficult goals. Now, what can I do for you? You looked like you needed some help."

"You're a *manager?*" the manager replied. "You mean you run a business? I didn't even know there *were* businesses in the ocean, or mermaids either."

"Well, who do you think runs things on this planet? Not humans!" She laughed at the very thought. "The Earth is three-fourths water after all. We leave it to you humans to manage things above the surface, and we take care of the rest. But recently we've noticed things aren't going all that well up here, what with global warming and wars and oil spills and so forth, so some of us do a little volunteer work on the side, to try to help humans out. Now, about that wish. What's on your mind?"

The manager hesitated. "It's not really that important. I just run one of the smaller units of a big company. I don't work on global issues." He looked at her apologetically.

"One drop at a time, as we say beneath the ocean," the mermaid answered with a smile and a toss of her dripping wet curls. "Besides, I *like* to solve small problems. They are ever so much easier than the big ones. So let's hear it! What's the matter?"

The manager took a deep breath.

"It's my workplace," he began. "There is something about the way we work and how we relate to each other and the attitudes people have. It's hard to explain, but I'm sure we could be doing better and working more closely together, and feeling a lot better about our work too. My people rarely take initiative and they aren't very enthusiastic. I'd say they don't really support my work as a manager, either. As a result, our performance isn't all that good and work often seems like a struggle—actually, like a losing battle.

"So I guess my wish is that I want us all to be more effective. I want things to be easier. And I want my people less dependent on me so I can count on them. I want to feel I'm not the only one worrying about the future or trying to improve things. And I'm sick of people giving me grief and complaining. They complain about everything—their jobs, the other people, their pay, their hours, me. And when something goes wrong, nobody wants to admit it and everyone starts laying the blame on someone else, and—"

"Okay, okay, I get the idea!" the mermaid interrupted with a chuckle, holding up a hand to stop him. "I'd certainly never want to work in a place like that. It sounds like your workplace drains people of their energy instead of energizing them. Is that right?"

"Yes, exactly. And I'm not even sure we are aware of it most of the time. But I really do wish there was a different way to work."

"Now you're talking!" the mermaid said. "Wishing for a better way to work is the first step in becoming a great manager. And now that we have a wish to work on, let's get started. I'll teach you how to transform your workplace into a better place to work. There *is* one condition, though."

"Condition?" the manager asked with concern. "What might that be?"

"That you never say, '*But . . .*' Agreed?"

"Never? Well, I guess that's not too hard."

"Wonderful!" the mermaid enthused. "I'll teach you everything I know about how to be a successful leader and how to make your workplace more positive and productive. Now let's see. I can't teach you everything in just one day. I think you'd better plan on coming back to the sea a few more times. Why don't you come back each weekend for the rest of the summer?"

"But I can't take that much time off. Things are already too out of control, and if I'm not there on Fridays, my employees are going to skip out too. Then we'll get even further behind. Besides, I sunburn too easily and saltwater gives me a rash."

"Are you forgetting your promise so soon?"

"What promise? Oh, not to say 'but.' But I—"

"But you can't take the time, yes, I know. That's how most humans feel. Then again, you don't have as long a tradition of management as we sea people do. We never try to take the time; we always *make* the time."

"I see. Actually, I don't see at all," the manager admitted.

"Well, it's a matter of deciding what's important—what is *most* important—and then scheduling yourself to do that thing first and foremost. Then anything else that is less important can come later if you have the time. If it is important to you to figure out how to turn your people around and help them achieve their full potential, then you will need to *make the time* to come here and work on it."

"But if . . . I mean, what if I do slip away to the beach each weekend, and my employees take advantage of my not being there? What if they start taking long weekends themselves?"

"A 'but' by any other name's the same," the mermaid said with a wink. "I've got a suggestion for you. Why not take a couple of days off in the middle of the week instead of the weekend? Then you won't have to fight the traffic to get here, and you can be in the office on Fridays and Mondays to play traffic cop to your employees, if you feel that's important too."

"But—I mean, *except* if I take weekdays off, then I won't be at the office to take care of paperwork and answer questions and make sure nobody makes any serious mistakes. My cell phone doesn't even work when I'm here!"

"You certainly sound indispensable. Maybe that's part of the problem. What do you think?"

"It *is* the problem, at least in a way," the manager replied. "I feel like I can't count on my employees to care enough or to do a consistently good job without me there to keep an eye on them. I spend so much of my time making sure they do *their* jobs well that I'm not even sure what *my* job is anymore. Maybe I *am* nothing more than a glorified traffic cop."

"We don't have roads under the sea, but from what I've heard, traffic cops aren't nearly as important as they may think they are. Most of the time you humans manage to drive your cars safely without someone telling you what to do. My guess is that drivers rely much more on their own judgment and the feedback they get through their own senses than they do on traffic cops. Is that right?"

"I suppose so, although I've never thought about it that way. Most of the information you need for driving does come through your own senses. You watch the road and the traffic, and you glance down occasionally at your speedometer or check that the turn signal is on when it's supposed to be. So yes, drivers work mostly off the information they get continually as they drive, and only need to be directed or corrected every now and then. You may not realize it if all you do is swim, but driving is a dangerous activity and we have to trust other drivers to take responsibility for their actions."

"Do you trust your employees to drive themselves to work without continuous supervision?"

"I see where you're going with this one!" the manager laughed. "Yes, I do trust them with the life-and-death decisions involved in driving to and from work. But no, I don't trust them to do their work without me maintaining control. And you're right about my time too. I keep saying I want to figure out how to improve things, but I never take—I mean *make*—the time to do anything about it. I guess the first step is simply to make the commitment to work on my goal instead of just complaining!

"Good! Now you're sounding like a leader, not just a manager."

"Okay, I'll see you next Wednesday. No ifs, ands, or buts."

"'Buts' are a hard habit to give up," the mermaid said with a smile. "However, I believe you will try your best, which is all anyone can ask. And you certainly *mean* well, which is a great start. Yes . . . I guess I'll take a gamble on you."

"Take a *gamble* on me?" the manager responded indignantly. "What do you mean? You make it sound like you're deciding whether to accept me into some special program or not."

"Ah, but I am!" the mermaid replied. "When was the last time you heard of a sea person giving lessons to a mere human being? It's quite an honor, as a matter of fact, and I don't want to waste it on someone who misses his appointments and doesn't pay attention. If you are going to be my pupil, then I will expect you to not only practice what you learn, but also pass it on to others. There are far too many human beings in the world for me to teach each and every one of them myself."

"Agreed," the manager said. "And now that we have an understanding, what is my first lesson?"

"You humans certainly are in a hurry," the mermaid laughed. "Perhaps it has something to do with being mortal. Well, since you insist, we'll start right away. Your first lesson is to walk back down the beach and collect some gifts for your employees. And while you are at it, why don't you help your daughter too. Isn't that little girl in the blue bathing suit yours?"

The manager squinted down the long stretch of beach, and nodded.

"She's looking for sea glass, and it's pretty hard to find," the mermaid told him. "Why don't you help her?"

"You want me to walk along the beach picking up stuff to give people? But I thought you were going to teach me about *leadership!*"

"What was that promise you made?"

The manager sighed. "No 'buts,' I know. But . . ."

"Have you ever heard of beach combing? That's what you need to do *right now.* I'd help you, except I . . ." She pointed to her long silvery tail and shrugged apologetically. "I guess legs are better for *some* things," she added. "Well, goodbye!" And with a flick of her tail and a swish of her long, dark tresses, she slipped into a rising wave and was gone.

"Hey!" the manager yelled in a sudden panic. "But when will I see you again?"

There was no answer from the seemingly endless sea.

2. Reflections

The manager stared at the sea for a long time, wondering if what he'd just seen was real or only a figment of his imagination. Then he shrugged and decided that he might as well do what the mermaid had said. After slipping his shoes off and wriggling his toes in the sand, he headed down the beach to join his daughter and see what treasures the ocean had cast up.

A couple of hours later, his daughter had filled her bucket with sea glass and the manager had filled his pockets with an assortment of small treasures: a sand dollar perfectly intact, smooth oval stones in many colors, and an interesting selection of shells and other salty treasures, all of which he planned to share with his employees when he got back.

As, laden with their newfound riches, he and his daughter walked quietly along the beach, the manager's worries began to return. He realized that he felt rather awkward about bringing his employees these gifts.

First of all, he was not in the habit of giving them gifts of any kind, and was not quite sure what he would say and how he would explain his actions. Moreover, of what value were these beach treasures in an office? His employees might prefer something more substantial if he was going to start giving them gifts.

He was debating whether to follow through with the plan when his young daughter resolved his dilemma by saying, "Don't worry about it, Daddy. At least they'll know you're thinking of them, and that's what counts, isn't it?"

"Exactly! What a clever child!" the mermaid's voice interrupted, surprising them. "The child has put her fin—I mean finger—on the key point of this lesson, hasn't she?"

The manager was not sure he knew what the key point was, but his daughter smiled at the mermaid and said, "You remind me of my kindergarten teacher. She told us the first rule of school was to take care of each other. Are you my daddy's teacher?"

"Yes, dear, and you are absolutely right. The first point I want to share with your father is that to have his wish come true, he needs to have a more *considerate* workplace. That's why I suggested he bring some shells back to share with his employees. The best way to create a more considerate workplace is to be more caring yourself, so that others will follow your example."

The mermaid went on to explain what she meant by a considerate workplace. She told the manager that to create exceptional spirit and encourage great performance, you must first create a caring community.

Later that day, in his hotel room, the manager made some notes to help him remember what she had said. Soon, he had created this list:

- *In a considerate workplace, people feel care and respect for one another and make an effort to be supportive.*

- *In a considerate workplace, people take a cooperative approach and look out for one another's interests, not just their own.*

- *A workplace in which everyone looks out for other people's needs is a healthy, nurturing place to work. It energizes its people instead of tiring them out.*

- *Consideration breaks down an "us-versus-them" mentality and builds a spirit of real teamwork.*

- *In a considerate workplace, people take the time to listen to one another and stop to make sure everyone is on board. They know that their success depends on everyone feeling willing and able to contribute.*

The list helped the manager recall some of the mermaid's suggestions on how to help create a spirit of consideration. She had told him that when sea people greet each other, they take longer to ask *"How are you?"* because they genuinely want to know the answer. In a considerate workplace, she said, people are more aware of one another's feelings. "As you are the manager," she explained, "it's your job to know how your people are feeling about their work, since to achieve your wish, you need your people to be feeling enthusiastic, not worried or frustrated."

He also recalled her observation that humans tend to *tell* more than *ask*, especially when they have a problem or disagreement. The manager had asked what that meant, and she explained that when people listen to each other more carefully, they find it easier to work out problems and so their workplace naturally becomes more considerate.

She recommended that the manager make a point of *asking more questions*—and now he made a note to himself about that too. In fact, he drew a big question mark with a blue felt-tipped pen on the back of a large white clam shell, and decided to keep the shell on his desk to remind him to ask questions more often.

Back at the beach, the manager had been uncertain about the mermaid's suggestion that he try to listen to his employees more. He had pointed out that he was happy to listen to *some* of his employees, but that others might take advantage of it and he didn't want to spend all his time listening to them gripe. So the mermaid had explained that in a considerate workplace, *everyone* listens well, and as a manager he had to teach his people that lesson. If an employee spent so much time talking about personal problems that he or she couldn't listen to the needs of others, then the manager had to ask that person to listen better too. For instance, the manager might request that the employee take some time to ask others about their situations or constraints, to better understand their viewpoints.

That evening, during the drive home, the manager's mind returned to his conversation with the mermaid, and lingered on his favorite part.

"I'm very impressed by your efforts to understand what I am saying," she had told him. "Your willingness to listen and be open-minded about new ideas is great."

"Am I receiving a compliment from a mermaid?" the manager exclaimed in surprise. "That's certainly a first for me!"

"Recognition does feel good, doesn't it?" she replied. Then she pointed out that in a considerate workplace, people often *encourage* one another's efforts and *thank* others for their contributions.

The manager said that in his workplace, recognition depended on good results and was given through bonuses and awards dinners. The mermaid seemed unimpressed and explained that consideration was different. It was a daily practice, and it focused on recognizing effort and progress more than end results.

"I never realized consideration and thoughtfulness were so important," the manager murmured to himself as he watched the road. "It seems so simple. But now that I think about it, people *do* always respond well to kindness. And everyone likes to work in a friendly environment where people look out for each other."

"Are you talking to yourself again?" his daughter asked him sleepily from the back seat of the car. "Why do you always think about your work?"

Feeling duly chastised, the manager turned his mind to more immediate concerns, and told his daughter a story to help her fall back to sleep. The story started out as an exciting adventure in which a young girl is kidnapped by pirates, but escapes from their ship with the help of a mermaid. Somehow, though, the mermaid and the girl ended up going back to the ship and teaching the pirate captain to be nice. They then reformed the management of his crew so that the ship would run more efficiently and profitably.

Fortunately, the manager's daughter had drifted off to sleep by that point in the story.

The manager wondered if perhaps his daughter was right—maybe he did think about his work all the time. But how could he avoid it? One problem or another was always looming in his mind. "Maybe," he thought, "things will be different now that I've learned about the power of consideration."

A loud honking startled him. Reminded of the busy highway under his wheels, he noticed a passing school bus full of laughing, joking children. Some of them waved to him and signaled a "V" for victory; others tossed soccer balls around. Most seemed to be girls, and one in particular, dressed in muddy sports gear, gave him an exuberant thumbs up as the bus pulled away. On its rear hung a banner: "Manchester Mermaids: Girls Junior All-Stars!"

"Must be on their way back from a big team victory" the manager thought. "Too bad we don't have that sort of spirit in my workplace."

He remembered the teams that he had formed over the course of various projects, and how so often they functioned like teams in name only. "Maybe we don't need teams so much as team*work*," the manager thought. "If I make an effort to be more considerate and thoughtful—to be a better listener too—and I encourage my people to make a similar effort, maybe teamwork will naturally develop." Whatever the result, it had to be better than when teamwork was dictated through formal assignments.

The manager was excited to have begun a new journey and eager to start practicing what he had learned. But he also was a little nervous about what he might find when he got back to the office, and how long it might take to see some real benefits from his new ideas.

He was also unsure how he would explain these ideas to his people. He had a feeling they would think he'd lost his mind if he told them he was taking lessons from a mermaid.

Up ahead, the school bus was still in view. Only now did the manager think of its banner.

3. Storm Warning

W hen the manager returned to his company on Tuesday morning, his first instinct was to bury himself in the office and catch up on his paperwork. But then he remembered his discussion with the mermaid. Perhaps it would be a better idea to catch up on his *people* work first. To find out, he made a point of visiting each of his employees to ask them how they were doing and what had happened in his absence. He told them he'd been thinking of them and hoping everything was going well, and he gave each of them one of the little gifts he'd collected from the sea.

He also told them he had returned from his vacation with the conviction that a more considerate workplace would be a good thing, and shared his personal goal of trying to be more thoughtful and supportive.

He didn't mention the mermaid.

To the manager's surprise, his employees reacted favorably, even enthusiastically, to his new way of thinking. Everyone *liked* the idea of a workplace where people were more caring and considerate and tried to look out for one another's interests. And he was not the only one who preferred to have less conflict and more support and cooperation in the workplace. Quite a few employees even thanked him for bringing the subject up and said they would make an effort to move the workplace in that direction.

His employees were also touched that he had thought to bring them some mementos from his trip. There were a few jokes about how next time they'd prefer pirate gold or an all-expenses-paid vacation, but the humor was good-natured, and he could tell they were surprised and pleased by his sincerity.

The manager realized that these people had no idea how much he cared about them or that they often crossed his mind when he wasn't around. Then again, he thought, how *would* they know, since he'd never told them?

All in all, it was one of the manager's best days ever. He sensed a new warmth and hopefulness in the office, and realized that his moods and actions probably had a far bigger influence on employee attitudes than he'd ever imagined. He left work on Tuesday almost caught up on his paperwork—and feeling pretty good about his people-work too.

He made himself a handy little sign to remind him of what this experience had taught him about management:

Peoplework
before
Paperwork!

But a good day, no matter how good, could never have prepared the manager for the shock awaiting him on Wednesday morning.

It came in the form of an innocent-looking manila envelope from headquarters, bearing the return address of the senior vice president to whom he reported. He should have known it was trouble when he cut his finger trying to tear it open.

Inside was a brief memo labeled "CONFIDENTIAL." It reviewed the poor recent performance of all the units in his division, and said that the company was exploring the possibility of moving all their work to subcontractors with lower labor costs. In the short term, the memo went on, headquarters would be looking for significant cost cuts and performance gains.

Moreover, while it was not yet certain, if the economy continued as it had in the recent past, he *might* be instructed to lay off his employees and shut his facility down.

The memo warned that this information was intended for his eyes only, and that he was strongly advised not to let the rumor of impending layoffs reach his workers. He should begin thinking about how to handle the transition, in case a layoff did prove necessary, and design a confidential plan in his spare time so his unit would be ready.

Finally, his boss said not to worry because even if his unit was closed, there would probably be a job for him at headquarters.

The manager found this final message far from reassuring. In fact, it irritated him that his boss would think his only concern was for himself. And the whole approach grated against his newfound enthusiasm for consideration. Was it considerate, he asked himself, to make plans that might hurt his employees and not even mention it to them? If he were in their shoes, wouldn't he want to know as early as possible that the unit might be heading for some rough times?

The manager felt terribly upset.

"Why does this have to happen now," he muttered, "just when I thought I might be able to start making a real difference?"

A bolt of anger flashed through him. Down his fist came, slamming his desk—and toppling an old cup of coffee there. It spilled over the memo as the manager reared back, knocking his chair over. The coffee was still dripping from the desktop's edge, onto the light beige carpeting, when his office door cracked open.

"Is there anything wrong?" his assistant asked, anxiously looking in.

"As a matter of fact, yes. More than you could possibly imagine. Could you bring me some paper towels?" He tacked on a hurried "Please?" as he belatedly recalled his vow to be more considerate.

Once he'd cleaned up the mess as best as he could, the manager closed the door to his office and held all calls that morning. This was something he needed to think through right away. He was scheduled to lead a staff meeting in just a few hours and he wanted to figure out what his approach would be.

What could he do? How should he handle it?

His boss, he knew, expected him to keep his cards close to the chest and give no hint of his concerns or feelings about the bombshell that had just exploded in his hands. And he suspected there might be some legalities connected to how the company notified employees in the eventuality of a layoff. He had no desire to stir up legal trouble. Yet he knew that it would be extremely inconsiderate not to share the news that the unit was in peril. He also knew that, if he were in his employees' situation, he would rather be involved in planning how to handle the problem than be left out.

These thoughts fought within him, and he could not make up his mind about what to do. "How come," he said to himself, "there's never a mermaid around when you really need one?"

The manager did his best to concentrate on the problem and avoid distractions, remembering the mermaid's advice to make time for top priorities. His assistant kept sticking his head in the door to ask if he could talk to callers, but the manager told him to schedule them for later in the week.

The company's new computer network proved harder to put off. The computer on his desk began beeping to warn him that he had an urgent e-mail message. Irritated, he pulled up the control panel on the screen and turned the volume all the way down.

The machine was silent for a few minutes. Then it began to emit a faint series of sounds he'd never heard from it before, rather like waves breaking on a gentle shore.

The wave sounds grew louder.

And louder.

Now it sounded like a storm surge against a rocky peninsula.

The manager cursed and turned the screen toward him, preparing to track down this new irritant and turn it off too. But to his surprise, the screen was full of fish swimming to and fro, and in the middle of it all floated a small bubble-like message window. It was definitely not from his e-mail program, and he had never seen anything like the sender's Web address (a long chain of cryptic characters linked by the occasional intelligible phrase, such as "gill.net," "fluke.sea," and "atlantis.gov"—all of which seemed oddly out of place on dry land). There was just a single sentence to the e-mail itself, which read:

> "When the water gets rough,
> see how far consideration will take you."

Well, the water certainly was getting rougher. And if this morning's memo was any indication, storm warnings were in order for the coming months. He resolved to stick to his vow of being a considerate manager and to warn his people that there might be bad weather ahead. "I'd want to know right away if *my* job were in danger," he thought, "so it is only considerate to let them know too." Relieved to have reached a decision that he felt good about, he began to prepare a new agenda for the upcoming staff meeting.

He started to write it down on a pad of yellow paper, only to find it was wet with coffee stains. So he typed it up on the computer instead. It had stopped making those watery noises and seemed to be back to normal, whatever exactly that was. Here is what he wrote:

How to Create a Considerate Workplace

✓ Lead *people,* not employees.

✓ Show by your actions that each member of the team matters.

✓ Let people know you care about them.

✓ Bring communication to a more honest and respectful level.

He hoped that with these principles as a starting point, he would find a way to "weather the storm" and lead his group to success.

4. Faith in the Tide

The days flew by, and soon it was time for the manager to return to the sea for his next lesson. As he drove toward the beach, he reflected on the strange week he had just experienced.

The staff meeting had gone better than expected, but it had still been hard on all of them. To open the meeting, he offered an apology for having to share bad news, and then stated that it was inconsistent with the new emphasis on consideration not to tell them, right away, that their unit might be in jeopardy. He also shared his own dilemma, explaining that although there was as yet no official decision to downsize or close the unit, he felt uncomfortable keeping people in the dark until a decision was made.

His opening remarks concluded with his expressed hope that layoffs would prove unnecessary. But, he added, if things kept going the way they were, something of the sort was fairly likely to happen before the year's end.

There had been absolute silence in the room when he finished his remarks. Everyone just sat there looking at him, not sure what to say or how to react. Finally, Juanita, one of his oldest and most respected employees, broke the silence by saying how much she appreciated his sharing this news with all of them right away. "It's not how things are normally done in this company," she said, "and I know it must have taken real guts for you to let us in on the latest corporate rumors. I, for one, appreciate your honesty. It is one thing to *say* you want to be more considerate and caring, but quite another to actually *do* it in a tough situation like this."

A number of the other employees also thanked him for sharing the news. Later on, he realized that he had never been thanked for bad news before. That at least was something.

But by the end of the week, the office was more subdued than usual and people seemed to be bracing for the worst. A number of employees approached him to see if he would give them letters of recommendation, just in case it proved necessary to seek other employment. He sensed how difficult it must be for them to work under a cloud of uncertainty. He worried that in spite of his good intentions, sharing the bad news might lead to worse performance problems than usual—which, unfortunately, might actually increase the chances of the layoffs they hoped to avoid.

So it was in a subdued mood that the manager checked into the seaside hotel (now less crowded than on the weekend) and wandered down to the beach. Before too long, he found himself sitting on the same rock, staring at his own shoes in the sand and worrying about his work.

"Hey, come on!" the mermaid shouted, interrupting his thoughts. "I want to show you something. Follow me along the shore to where those rocks jut out into the sea."

The manager got up, pleased that the mermaid had kept their rendezvous, and walked to the end of the sandy beach.

"A little further—watch your footing," she told him, rolling and splashing along in the waves nearby. "Now, tell me what you see."

The manager looked around. "Rocks, and seaweed," he reported. "Nothing much, really. The tide's out so it's kind of dry."

"Yes," the mermaid replied. "In fact, to us sea-dwellers it is a desert. If we're caught out there at low tide, it can be deadly. But tell me what else you see. Is there anything living aside from the seaweed?"

"No, not really," the manager replied, looking around. "Except maybe in these little tide pools. Hold on, let me take a look."

He clambered down to a low spot in the rocks where a pool of ocean water had been left behind by the tide. Looking down into it, he was surprised to see it was crowded with creatures. There were snails and minnows and a small crab and a half-dozen starfish. The starfish were sitting quite still, clinging to the rocks. He was not even sure they were alive.

"Do you see them now?" the mermaid asked. "The pools along here are usually full of starfish. They aren't very fast, so the falling tide often catches them. But they don't worry about it; they just find a low spot in the rocks and hold on until the waves come back again."

"That's nice," the manager replied, not quite sure what the point of the story was.

"It's more than nice," the mermaid said, laughing. "It's life as opposed to death for those starfish. If they stayed out in the open air, they would die. In fact, if they had to live for more than a few hours in those little pools, they'd probably die too. But starfish don't panic or get depressed. They don't freak out or give up, because they have absolute faith. Living on the edge of the sea, starfish are born with the knowledge that the tide may go out, but *it will always come back in.*

So they realize that when the waves go out too fast or too far for them to follow, they simply have to find a tide pool and hold on until the water returns."

"Their strategy is to hold on and wait for better times?" the manager said. "Is there a lesson here?"

"What do *you* think?" the mermaid asked. "Do you ever have times when the tide is going out and you simply can't do anything to stop it?"

"Sure. That's pretty much what seems to be going on right now in my business," the manager said. "In fact I wanted to talk to you about that. Everyone is feeling pretty down and depressed at the moment, and I doubt that they'll be able to perform well under the circumstances."

"And you can't change the circumstances?"

"No, I don't think so. We're victims of trends in the economy, and our fate will ultimately be determined by the executives at headquarters. Which leaves everyone feeling, well, like they might be left high and dry."

"We sea people have a saying that goes, 'May Neptune grant me the wisdom to take control of those things that are in my power and to accept those things that are not.' When bad things happen, there are always some causes beyond our personal control. When it comes to the tide, well, that's entirely beyond our control, so it's an extreme example. In situations like that, the starfish knows to search for a tidepool, then hold on and hope for a change of tide. You see, even when something as inevitable as the tide is falling, there are still things you can do to improve your situation. The starfish never gives up and never lets go. Starfish are the ultimate optimists, and so they always survive."

The manager thought about his workplace. He didn't think it was a particularly optimistic place to be. As a matter of fact, it was surprising that his staff had simply accepted the bad news he'd given them in the last meeting. Nobody had even asked what they could do to try to avoid the disaster.

"I think right now my people are ready to just let go and be thrown against the rocks as soon as the first storm comes along," he said. "We aren't really that positive of a group. In fact, there is probably way too much negative thinking. We're a lot more capable and powerful than those little starfish, but because of our attitudes, we feel a lot more helpless than they do."

"Yes," the mermaid agreed with a warm smile. "What makes those starfish powerful is their *attitudes* and nothing else."

"I like the idea of focusing on attitudes," the manager said. "It seems to me that my people are getting discouraged and pessimistic, and that this is perhaps an even greater barrier for us than the economy. I don't want my people to feel helpless, especially when the tide is ebbing and we need every ounce of energy and ingenuity we have."

"That helpless feeling is your worst enemy in tough times," the mermaid agreed. "Here's an interesting question. What is the opposite of the word 'helpless'?"

"I guess it's something like 'in control,' 'in charge,' or 'able.' 'Capable,' maybe."

"Yes," the mermaid replied. "Those are powerful words for powerful feelings. Maybe *'powerful'* is a good word to express the opposite of 'helpless.' What do you think?"

"I like that word," the manager said. "I was going to say the opposite of 'helpless' is *'helpful,'* but I don't really think they're true opposites."

"Why not?" the mermaid asked. "People who feel helpful don't feel helpless, do they? If you can encourage people to help one another, then you can rest assured that they are not going to behave in a helpless manner. Acting helpful is one of the most powerful ways of combating helplessness and pessimism, and of stimulating good feelings instead. People always feel more cheerful and in control of their fate after they have helped someone else."

"Maybe we can get a more positive cycle of feelings going in my group by trying to be more helpful to one another as a starter," the manager said thoughtfully. "And that certainly is a natural next step to go along with consideration."

"Good idea," she said, then added, "As a manager, can you think of other ways to encourage a more positive attitude in your workplace too?"

"Well, I was wondering if I made a mistake by giving them bad news," the manager replied. "It seems to have *dis*couraged them."

"Any news is good news when it comes to management," the mermaid said. "You see, people get feeling down and discouraged and negative when they feel like they are out of control. And keeping them in the dark certainly limits their feeling of control. The more information they have, the more in control of their lives they feel; so information is good. On the other hand, how people *react* to information can make a big difference. As managers, we need to set a good example by reacting in a positive way to both good news and bad news."

The mermaid went on to explain that people usually exaggerate their bad news. If one bad thing happens, they talk about it as if it means many more bad things will inevitably happen. Soon they begin to think the sky is going to fall—specifically on them!

She recommended that the manager listen carefully to how his people *talk* about bad news, and that he intervene and offer an alternative view if need be. Saying things like "It is probably an isolated incident" and "It could have happened to anyone" help keep the news from discouraging people. This was important because he didn't want his people to get so depressed that they couldn't hang on or keep moving ahead.

She also urged the manager to ask his people to *think of ways to take control* and improve a bad situation or at least learn to avoid a bad result the next time.

"Of course, don't forget about *good* news," the mermaid said. "It's very important to use it to boost positive feelings as much as possible." She recommended celebrating every victory, no matter how small. "One achievement leads to another," she said. "And even a journey of a million miles must begin with a single swish of the tail."

"But," the manager objected, "sometimes there's not even one significant accomplishment or successfully completed project for me to recognize or for our group to celebrate. What then?"

"The most important achievement," the mermaid said, "is the *effort* to achieve. Whenever someone tries hard, you need to recognize their effort. Praise them for improvements, even if they fall short of the ultimate goal. Celebrate hard work in order to give everyone—including yourself—a pat on the back. The starfish is proud of its ability to cling to the rocks. It takes quiet pride in each minute that it hangs on and waits for the low tide to pass and the new water to flood in. Yet as managers we tend to forget to recognize effort and we find it hard to praise intermediary achievements. That is why under the water we always say that *the greatest achievement is the* effort *to achieve. It makes everything else possible.*"

"And by the way," the mermaid continued, "you need to be careful about your own language when you talk to yourself or your people. For instance, did you notice you broke your vow to me by saying 'but' just a moment ago? 'But' is a good example of negative talk. It usually leads to objections or reasons why *not.*"

The mermaid then talked with the manager about using positive talk, which she said is any talk that helps people see possibilities, bridge gaps, or feel better about themselves and others.

In positive workplaces, she said, people encourage the ideas of others and give one another *new ideas* all the time. They recognize one another's *strengths* instead of focusing on faults.

She also said that recognition was much more common in the most positive workplaces. Praise is mutual, and if nobody else is around to do the praising, people pat themselves on the back, congratulating themselves or allowing themselves a celebration.

"Now before you go," the mermaid told the manager, "there is one other sea creature I want to introduce you to."

She gave a loud whistle, and suddenly a graceful form leapt out of the water and splashed back down into it. Then the creature leapt out of the water again, this time holding itself in the air vertically by pumping its powerful tail so that it seemed to be walking on the water. With a gleeful laugh, it dove again and was gone.

"Was that a dolphin?" the manager asked.

"Yes," the mermaid replied. "I'm friends with quite a few of them, and I asked this one to stick around to give you a little demonstration. Did you notice anything special about what he did?"

"Well," the manager thought out loud, "he jumped clear out of the water and splashed back in. Then he danced above the waves. I guess that's pretty special, but don't dolphins do things like that all the time?"

"Exactly!" the mermaid replied with delight. "They are highly playful creatures. They don't actually *have* to jump and leap and play in the waves. They don't find fish above the water or anything practical like that. They just jump and play to feel good. Dolphins are the happiest creatures in the ocean."

"So they jump and play because they are happy?" the manager asked.

"No, not at all," the mermaid corrected. "It's really the other way around. They are happy because they play. They leap out of the water to cheer themselves up. It's their way of practicing being happy—their 'up exercise.' If they do it regularly, they find that they feel better and have more energy and get along better. Dolphins are very serious about feeling good. If they don't feel up, they think they are sick. And then the doctor sends them out to play."

> The tougher the situation, the more effort you need to put into keeping work **fun**!

"Wow," the manager said. "I guess feeling good is a serious project, at least for dolphins."

"It should be for managers as well," the mermaid said. "How can you expect your people to be up if *you* are feeling down and discouraged?"

"I guess I need to learn from the dolphin," the manager laughed. "I don't do enough 'up exercises,' nor do my people. I wonder what things we could do at the office to help everyone stay up despite the stress we're facing right now?"

"Good question!" the mermaid cried as she dove into a wave and slipped out of view. He watched the ocean for a while and thought he saw her leap out of a distant wave and splash back in.

A gust of wind blew his wet clothes against his body and made him shiver. The air was damper and cool now as the sun fell and the shadows lengthened. The manager realized he had better pack up and head back. "But first," he thought, "I think I'll just change into a dry shirt and sweater and go for a short walk along the beach. That will help me feel relaxed and happy enough to go back to work in a really positive frame of mind!"

He left the sea this time with a renewed enthusiasm for his group and its potential. That feeling was partly inspired by an assignment the mermaid had asked him to complete before going home. It involved taking a few minutes to make a list of five strengths for each of his employees.

His assignment had sounded simple enough, but as he sat in his hotel room, staring at a blank piece of Beachcombers Inn stationery, he found that it was awfully difficult. Gradually, though, he began to get the hang of it. He realized the difficulty was not with the assignment or his employees, but with his inclination to worry and imagine what could go wrong. Thus, although his employees had many strengths that he could list—and list them he eventually did—he'd began the assignment by trying to catch his employees' errors, unintentionally focusing on their *weaknesses* rather than their strengths. His perspective had been only negative.

Realizing this, the manager suspected that he might be partially responsible for the lack of positivity in his workplace. In fact, he rarely spoke to people about their strengths or thanked them for the special skills or positive attitudes they brought to the group. That would be his own assignment, he decided, and it ought to be a good place to start his campaign to create a more positive workplace where everyone focused on making things possible instead of arguing over what was *not* possible.

The mermaid had given him one more assignment too, but this one was for all of his employees, not just him alone. It was to *start making as long a list as possible of all the things they could do that might help them improve their situation.*

"You never know whether you can solve a problem until you *try,*" she had pointed out. "Maybe you and your people can't do anything to prevent your unit from closing down or having a major layoff. But then again, maybe you *can.* You simply don't know until you take the time to really think it through. In a positive workplace, people always start with the assumption that they *will* fix a problem. They truly believe anything is possible. And it is amazing how many times they succeed simply because their optimism gives them the energy to keep going until they uncover a hidden solution."

"I don't think we can change the economic forces or control what headquarters does," the manager said.

"Why don't you talk about what you think you *can* do," the mermaid replied. "Talk about the possibilities, not the impossibilities. A positive workplace is one in which people are positive that they *can* do things, not positive that they can't!"

And so the manager drove home thinking about how smart some of his people were, how calm or steady or funny or knowledgeable or well-spoken or kind others were, and about their many other strengths. He then thought about how he would ask them to come up with ideas for helping to avoid a layoff and ways of trying to revitalize their unit. "With all those strengths," he said to himself, "there must be *some* way we can improve the situation!"

BEACHCOMBERS INN

How to Have a
Positive Workplace

✓ Manage attitudes to maintain optimism. Focus on the good things that happen, not the bad.

✓ When bad things happen, stimulate a feeling of security by focusing on anything you *can* do to weather the storm or to improve the weather.

✓ Recognize effort and focus on strengths. (Otherwise you'll be recognizing failure and focusing on weaknesses!)

✓ Nurture a spirit of playfulness in yourself and your people. It turns problems into opportunities.

5. A Flood of Ideas

When the manager got back to the office, he called a staff meeting right away. His employees trickled in, looking more than a little discouraged. One of them made a half-hearted joke about how she couldn't wait for the next piece of bad news. Another said, "What, no shells this time?" There were a few chuckles at that, but the overall mood was pretty downtrodden. The manager noticed dark circles under many employees' eyes.

At the last moment, Juanita bustled in with two big boxes of donuts, followed by her assistant, James, who carried a large electric coffeepot. The manager's face lit up and so did almost everyone else's. "Thanks for thinking of us!" he told Juanita and James. "I guess I was so preoccupied with our problems, I forgot to be considerate."

"You were considerate enough last week to cover you this week too," Juanita told him. "And besides, what goes around comes around, as my grandmother always used to say,"

With a smile, she took her place at the conference table, and the meeting began.

The manager told his staff that he had not brought them anything tangible from the beach this time, but he *had* brought them the story of the starfish. He told them how the starfish has to face a falling tide twice each day, and how it always finds its way to a low spot on the rocks and holds on.

He suggested that they all think about where they could go and how they would hold on in case the worst were to happen and the whole unit was closed down. He asked each of them to come up with some ideas for alternative jobs, and to think about ways to begin cutting their personal expenses or increasing their savings.

"I am not asking you to take another job, because I am hopeful we will all pull through this together," he said. "However, I think we all need to find the emotional and economic strength to know we can 'hold on' and survive even if we do lose our jobs. So if that means taking a little personal time for planning, or enrolling in a course at the community college to increase your employability, or networking through friends and relatives to find out about options, then I want you to do that. And let's help each other out, too, by sharing information and getting together to encourage each other. Even if this place gets shut down entirely, I have faith that we can all hold on and survive the low tide. It could even turn out to be a strengthening experience for all of us as long as we remember that the tide will eventually come back in."

His employees were a little surprised by his suggestions and said they appreciated his willingness to help them prepare for the worst. They agreed to put some effort into being prepared and vowed to support one another and not to get discouraged if things did get worse in the coming months.

The manager then went on to say that he had been thinking about the possibility of their unit being closed down, and had realized that while it was certainly a threat to them all, it was *not* something they had to accept lying down. To illustrate this assertion, he told them about the dolphin and how it kept its spirits up.

He said that they needed to leap into action too.

Then he asked if anyone had thought about ways of minimizing the problem or even avoiding it. In answering that question, he said, he wanted them to follow just one rule. And that was to talk about things they *could* do, not things they could *not* do.

"I know there are a lot of things that are out of our control right now," the manager explained. "We can't change the economy or stem the tide of jobs moving to other countries with lower labor rates. But dwelling on those factors is like complaining about the tide going out. It won't help us and it will probably leave us feeling more discouraged and helpless than before. So let's try to focus on anything we *can* do that might help improve the situation, even if only a little bit. If we start showing improvements in our numbers, headquarters just might leave us alone."

Maybe it was the coffee and donuts, or maybe it was the manager's positive attitude, but soon everyone around the table was talking about ideas and sharing suggestions. In fact, the room began to grow louder and louder as different groups of employees began talking at the same time. The manager was about to call the meeting back to order, but Juanita placed a restraining hand on his arm and said, "Let them talk for a while. You don't want to nip their creativity in the bud." And so the manager sat back and waited until the conversation began to lag. Then he got up and went to the board with a red marker and asked them to share their ideas with the rest of the room.

There was a sudden silence, and the manager began to feel uncomfortable. Not wanting to stand there feeling dumb while nobody volunteered ideas, he quickly pointed at the nearest employee and said, "OK, Bill, why don't you start? Got any good ideas?"

Bill opened his mouth, then closed it. He shifted uncomfortably in his seat. Finally he shook his head and said, "No, not really."

The manager was surprised, but passed on to the next employee, who, fortunately, was more willing to speak. She suggested that they work on cutting overtime hours since those were so expensive. The manager wrote "Overtime hours?" on the board, then turned back to the employee and said, "But didn't we try to do that last year? What happened to that initiative? I thought we decided that overtime was cheaper than hiring more people."

The next employee didn't have a suggestion. Nor did the one after that. The manager wondered what had happened to all the energy and talk he had heard in the room a few moments before. He started to say something about how it was important for everyone to share their ideas, but was interrupted by the ringing of a cell phone.

"I thought we had a rule against bringing cell phones into staff meetings," he said. "Could whoever that is turn their phone off please?"

But the phone kept on ringing, louder now.

"I think it's coming from your briefcase," his assistant said to him.

The manager checked.

It was.

"I thought I'd turned that phone off," he muttered, grabbing it and holding the off-button down hard.

The phone kept ringing.

Puzzled, the manager hit the talk button and held the phone to his ear. All he could hear was the gentle sound of breaking waves and the cry of sea gulls.

Then he heard the mermaid's voice.

She said, "I forgot to tell you that when you encourage a more positive attitude, you also have to encourage creativity. Creativity and positive thinking go flipper to flipper. You are going to need lots of creative ideas to improve your situation."

"I *know* we need ideas," the manager said a little irritably. "I'm trying to lead an idea session right now as a matter of fact. Can you call me later?"

"How do your people feel about sharing their ideas with you?" the mermaid asked, ignoring his hurried tone of voice.

"I don't know how they feel," the manager said, "and I really have to go now, if you'll excuse me."

"If you don't know, why don't you *ask* them?" the mermaid suggested.

"Ask them *what?*" the manager said, but all he heard in reply was the whistle of the sea wind and the gurgle of the ocean waves. He looked at his cell phone again. The power still seemed to be off, but the window display showed a bed of clams on the sea floor, their strong white shells clamped tightly shut.

He dropped the phone back in his briefcase, and realized everyone was staring at him.

"Who was that?" Juanita asked him.

"Oh, um, sorry about that. Just a friend calling."

"A friend who asks you about the meeting you're running? There's something a little fishy about that," Juanita kidded him.

"More fishy than you think," the manager muttered. "Let me ask you a question. How do you feel about my asking you for your ideas? I mean, is everyone comfortable with that?"

There was an awkward silence. The manager sensed that behind their stares they were all wondering if he was going to bite them.

He was about to fill the silence himself when he caught the faint sound of waves coming from his briefcase again. It distracted him for long enough that a new employee named James spoke up instead.

"Nothing personal," he said, "but honestly, I feel a little nervous about telling you my ideas. I mean, it's not like we have thought out our plans or have any clear proposals in mind. We were just throwing ideas around. They might sound pretty stupid to you."

"Oh," the manager said. He hadn't thought that his employees could be embarrassed to share their ideas with him. "I see. But I don't mean to pass judgment on your ideas. I just want to get a lot of thoughts out in the open to get us started."

"Well, if you don't mind my saying so," Bill volunteered, speaking up for the first time, "it sometimes sounds like you *are* judging our ideas. For instance, you remember when you asked me if I had any ideas? What you actually said is do I have any *good* ideas. And I wasn't sure whether you'd think my ideas were good or not. I always have ideas, but unless I have the time to work them into formal proposals, I don't feel ready to defend them in front of the boss."

The manager nodded, realizing that he had been misunderstood. "Oh, I see," he replied. "But that's not what I really meant. You can feel free to speak in front of me. Any other comments?"

Silence descended on the room again. The manager shifted uncomfortably in his seat. Finally he said, "Well, maybe we've done enough for one day. Shall we break up and try again next week?"

"Okay's" and "I guess so's" were murmured around the table as people began to collect their papers and coffee cups.

"Excuse me," Juanita said, "but I think there are actually a lot of great ideas we raised today that we need to write down and discuss. If we wait until next week, we may forget them, and we'll certainly lose some valuable time.

"I also think you need to know," she continued, giving the manager a firm look, "that while you don't mean to, you often *do* shut down the discussion. For one thing, each time one of us tries to answer a question, you immediately argue back. I know you don't mean to, but it often sounds like you are debating what we said. If you want to really listen to what we have to say, then just listen. If your employees sense that you are reacting at all defensively, they will clam up since nobody wants to argue with the boss—even a nice boss like you!"

"But I—"

The manager stopped. He realized he was about to debate Juanita's observation that he was debating what people said. He also realized he was saying "but" a lot. That sounded like a violation of the mermaid's injunction and a clear example of negative talk.

The manager began to say, "You may be right," but stopped himself. That was more positive, but it still involved him passing judgment on Juanita's comment. He thought that if he wanted his employees to share their ideas freely, he would have to stop passing judgment on everything they said. Juanita was right, the manager realized. He had shut their idea session right down without even meaning to. It was hard to lead a free airing of ideas in his role as the boss.

Suddenly, he realized he didn't really have to! Turning to Juanita, he said, "I'm not very experienced at leading idea sessions, and in my role as the boss, it's too easy for me to inhibit people's ideas without even meaning to. So how's this for an idea, Juanita. If everyone is willing to stay a little longer, why don't *you* lead the session and collect as many ideas as you can? I can leave the room if you like, or I can just switch seats with you and keep my mouth shut for a while."

Juanita smiled and said, "If it's all right with everyone else, I'd be happy to give it a try. And I'd prefer it if you stayed in the room and contributed your ideas too. Here, let me have that marker. Now, the only thing I think we need to agree on is that we won't critique any of the ideas people share. In fact, I'd like to write down any and every idea we can, including obviously silly ones."

"Why waste our time on stupid ideas?" someone asked from the far end of the conference room.

"One idea can lead to another," Juanita replied. "For instance, when we were all talking earlier, James said as a joke, 'Why don't *we* subcontract our work overseas before headquarters can do it to us?' The idea made us laugh and wasn't meant seriously. But it got me thinking that we probably *could* subcontract a few of the things we do here, if not overseas at least to a specialized firm in this country. For example, we're old-fashioned in the way we handle all customer calls through our main switchboard. A lot of newer companies use specialized call-centers to handle their routine service calls. So it gave me the idea that we might be able to find a firm that could handle a lot of our calls for us at a cheaper cost per call. And if so, that would allow us to focus on the more challenging high-value activities that we have a hard time getting done because we're always being interrupted by the phone."

"Hey, that's not a bad idea," the manager burst out enthusiastically. "I bet we—" The water sounds from his briefcase rose in volume, interrupting him again. "Sorry," he said hastily, hoping the sounds would stop before anyone else noticed. "I didn't mean to critique your suggestion now, Juanita. However, maybe I could suggest another idea that yours made me think of. You know how we spend a lot of time preparing monthly mailings? That is also something we might be able to subcontract."

Juanita turned and jotted the idea down on the whiteboard behind her.

"What about using the Internet to send out notices or bills, and getting rid of the paper mailings?" someone else said.

Juanita nodded to show she understood and quickly jotted that idea down too.

"I was thinking we might . . ."

"What about . . ."

Ideas began to flow so fast that Juanita was writing continually.

At first everyone was fairly serious, but then someone made a joke, and when Juanita wrote that down too, the group loosened up and began suggesting anything that came to mind. Amazed at how many ideas they had, the manager sat back and watched. Soon the board was almost full, and he slipped out of his seat to fetch a flip pad on a stand.

Juanita switched over to the pad and kept writing. Employees were suggesting new ways to handle the work flow, new flex-time options to reduce their commutes (in which they would split the saved time between home and work, thereby working an extra 15 minutes each day), ideas for preventing errors and improving quality, and lots of suggestions for cutting costs.

One employee said she thought the building was usually too cold when the air-conditioning was on, and several others agreed. Then someone said it was hotter where he worked, near the copy machines, but that if he could have a fan at his workstation, he wouldn't mind the AC being turned down either. Another employee said that the fluorescent panel lights throughout the building must be expensive, and what if they turned those off on sunny days and let people who weren't near a window use desk lights instead? Another person suggested getting a bin for returnable bottles and cans, since most people threw them into the recycling pile now. Once a week someone could bring them to a return station and collect the change. It might not be much, but if they saved it up, they could probably use it to buy inexpensive desk lamps.

The ideas kept flowing until Juanita's list filled multiple pages, and James went to get some tape to put the ideas up around the room.

Finally, everyone began to tire and the ideas slowed down to a trickle.

"Here's a suggestion, Juanita," the manager said. "There are so many great ideas here that I think we should save them. Let's transfer the ones on the board to paper, and keep them and all the others posted around the room. This can become our Op Center for our turnaround, and we can keep working on these ideas as we go and adding to them whenever anyone wants."

"Great idea!" Juanita said enthusiastically. "Not that I mean to pass judgment on any of the suggestions, of course, but we do need to decide where we go from here. What do you think we should do next? Any thoughts on how to start implementing some ideas?"

The room fell quiet again.

"Well, it seems to me that we—or at least I—have learned a useful lesson today," the manager said. "We had to adopt a completely open approach to get all these ideas out in the first place, and I think most of them are going to need more work before we can begin to implement them. Maybe we should continue to use a participatory style as we develop these ideas. I don't think I'm ready to take over and implement these ideas by myself. How do you feel about forming some teams and letting each team work on the ideas they like best?"

"Well, what do you say?" Juanita asked the group from her position by the flip chart. "Do you think we could put together some teams and get some projects going?"

"If it means we might be able to save our own rears," Bill said, "I'm all for it. But I think my supervisor is going to want me back at my desk pretty soon."

"*I'm* his supervisor," Juanita explained with a grin, "and as far as I'm concerned, anyone who wants to take some time during the day to work on our survival plans should be able to." She turned to the manager. "What do *you* think?" she asked.

The manager thought how far behind they might get if everyone started spending their time sitting around the conference room talking. But then he remembered how he had asked the mermaid to help him create a more positive workplace, one where everyone pitched in and took initiative to solve problems. If he didn't support these people now, he thought, he might never get his wish.

"I agree, and I'm excited that you want to work on solving our problems," the manager said. "But I'm also a bit anxious about what will happen if we fall behind on our routine work while we try to improve our costs and quality. If our monthly performance figures slip in the short term, we may be sending the wrong signal to headquarters. So I'm not quite sure how to answer your question."

There was silence again as everyone digested this thought. This time, however, the manager decided to keep quiet and wait for a response instead of jumping in to fill the silence.

"I'm learning!" he told himself. "And all along I thought it was my *people* who had to do the learning."

Finally, Bill spoke up. "I think hurting short-term results is a significant risk," he said, "but instead of letting it stop us, let's just add it to our list of problems to solve. I'm willing to be on a team that focuses on how we cover our short-term work at the same time we work on new ideas. Will anyone else join me?"

"Good idea!" several people said at once. One of the employees pointed out that her department usually had a lighter schedule than the others in the summer, and could probably cover for some of the other employees while they worked on special projects. Someone else suggested that they might be able to cut back efforts on long-term projects like maintenance and converting to new software, since these projects weren't going to affect their monthly results or help them turn the unit around by the end of the year anyway.

Soon a group had formed to make sure the other teams could put time into developing the turnaround ideas without hurting short-term results. They asked Bill to be the point person, and he agreed that anyone who ran into trouble or ran out of time trying to work on turnaround ideas should contact him so that his team could step forward and help.

Someone suggested that Juanita should be the point person for the other turnaround teams, and the manager added his vote to her nomination, pleased to see that natural leaders were emerging.

"One final thing," the manager said as they were about to break up and go back to work. "A friend of mine told me that when you have too much to do, you have to decide what your most important project is and *take the time for it* first. I suggest that we treat our turnaround efforts as our most important project. If that means your team wants to come in here and meet for an hour when you get to work, that's fine by me and it should be fine with your supervisors too. If we don't *take* the time to work on this effort, we certainly won't *find* the time, because we're all pretty busy as it is. Agreed?"

"Yes, but who's going to handle my calls while I sit in a meeting?" someone asked.

"That would be our problem," Bill spoke up. "If you want my group to work on it, just come by my desk later today and we'll see what we can come up with. Maybe we can route your calls to people who *are* at their desks, and then have you cover their calls when they are in here working on their projects."

The manager smiled a big smile. "Initiative," he thought. "Commitment too. And caring. Plus creative problem-solving and positive thinking and consideration for one another and a collaborative spirit! What a nice place to work this is becoming."

And then he thought, "I sure hope it's not too late. I'd hate to see us get shut down just when we are really coming together as a team."

6. Opportunities

It was another beautiful day at the beach, and the manager felt lucky to be able to call what he was doing work. He had walked down to the rocks to get a close-up look at a starfish. It was the mermaid's idea. She said she wanted to teach him some marine biology. The manager was skeptical of that, however, and suspected it was her way of sharing the next lesson with him.

"The starfish feels its way across the ocean floor," the mermaid said. "Its five arms are covered with sensors. They are even more sensitive than the skin on your fingers. So in a way, the starfish is almost all hand. It gets so much information with each movement that it is very sensitive to its environment."

The manager leaned down to pick up a small starfish from the rocks at his feet. "Hey, it's stuck," he said. "I can't get it off the rock. It's surprisingly strong!"

"That's the other thing about the starfish I wanted to tell you," the mermaid replied. "Its arms are almost pure muscle, and as it travels it is constantly exercising them. Its lifestyle naturally strengthens it. Did you know that starfish grow continually? That one there, it's small now, but it will grow a little each year. They never stop growing."

"Is this another one of your lessons?" the manager asked suspiciously.

"Two lessons in one, since you are always in such a hurry," the mermaid teased him. "To have your wish and create the wonderful workplace you want—"

"*Need,*" the manager interrupted, thinking about the threat of closure hanging over all of them.

"Yes, to get the workplace you need," the mermaid said, "you have to make sure it is both highly informed and strengthening."

"Informed as in lots of information?" the manager asked.

"Yes, but what I really mean is that everyone there needs to be well informed about *their work* at all times."

"But aren't they? We have performance reviews, and we circulate the monthly sales figures and the quarterly profit and loss figures. And everyone has access to the Internet if they want to catch up on the latest news or whatever."

"There is a big difference," she said, "between providing information on the one hand, and making sure everyone is informed about their work on the other. For instance, how much of the information on the Internet right now is helpful to an employee who wants to know exactly how well they are performing?"

The manager shrugged.

"None. So that leaves the annual performance reviews. Do employees find those useful to look at on a regular basis as they try to improve their productivity or cut costs or do whatever else you need to do to keep your unit open?"

"Well . . . not really. In fact, I think the performance reviews are kept on file in the HR department, so it would be kind of hard to read them regularly. Besides, they don't go into that level of detail. What you're talking about is feedback, right?"

"Yes, at least partly. But a lot of managers assume feedback means the boss tells the employee whether they did a job well or poorly. That keeps the employee dependent on the boss's approval, and you told me you want employees who are independent and take initiative to improve their own performances, right?"

"Of course."

"So what you need is to help employees understand and judge their own work more clearly. You need to help them get access to *informative* feedback. They need to be able to track their own progress easily. That's why you want to make your workplace a highly informed one."

"Okay, I'll get right to work on that," the manager said with enthusiasm. "There's just one thing, though. I have no idea how."

"Let's look at the way the starfish finds food." the mermaid suggested. "It often feeds in dark water, and so must feel its way carefully over the sea floor. Through its five arms, it constantly receives detailed information about what it's finding there. If the starfish feels something bad, it moves away. If it feels something good, it moves toward it. Work is often like dark water because you so often have to work 'in the dark' on things that are complex and hard to see.

"If all you have to do is something simple like hit a nail with a hammer," she continued, "then you can keep an eye on the nail and adjust your swing if you aren't hitting the nail square on. But in work, and in life in general, we often must do things that aren't so simple or easy to see. The idea is to figure out ways of collecting information easily and quickly so we can feel our way along despite the fact we can't always see the head of the nail we want to hit."

This made sense to the manager, and brought a memory to mind. "I remember once when I worked as a factory supervisor, we taught the line employees to check their work every hour or so and keep a log of it. They only had to mark an 'X' on a graph next to their machines to record their latest measurement. At first they grumbled about taking the time out to collect the data. But once they got used to it, they loved it. They could tell right away if something was slipping out of adjustment, then fix it themselves, before anything went seriously wrong or any bad products left the line. They never had to shut down the line or do rework. And you wouldn't believe the amount of time and money they saved the company, just from using that simple measurement technique."

"That's a good example of making a workplace more informed," the mermaid said, highly pleased. "And it can happen in any workplace, not only a factory. All you have to do as the manager is help employees figure out what information they need in order to track their own work quality. For instance, someone who takes customer service calls might want to keep a simple record of the mood of each caller. Are they mad, upset, unfriendly, or are they happy, friendly, grateful? Once someone starts noticing and recording a little piece of information like that, it can have an amazing impact on their performance."

"I'd love to be able to review my employees' performances by knowing whether their customers are happy or not," the manager said. "But I doubt they'd want to share that information with me unless they cheated and gave themselves high ratings all the time."

"It's not information for *you*," the mermaid laughed. "We're talking about informed *employees*, not informed managers. The information you need is very different. What you need to know is *whether they have all the information they need to evaluate their own performances*. That way, you don't have to do it on a regular basis anymore. I thought you wanted independent employees, right?"

"Yes," the manager agreed. "But typical management methods seem to make employees dependent instead. It's hard to break the habit."

"Here's a good way to motivate yourself to give employees the power to improve their own performances. Remember that you are taking yourself out of the feedback loop every time you find a way to give employees direct feedback about their work. Which frees you up for more important things. Like saving your ship. Didn't you tell me it's about to sink?"

"It's not a ship, it's a unit of a company," the manager corrected. "But yes, there is a real danger we might sink unless we improve our results in a hurry."

"Great!" the mermaid said with a smile. "I always like a good challenge. Speaking of which, do you remember what your second lesson of the day is?"

"The workplace needs to be more informed, and, and . . ."

"And it needs to be strengthening for the people who work in it," the mermaid helped out. "You see, in too many workplaces, people feel like they're getting used up. Their work wears them out and runs them down. But in the kind of workplace you wished for, everyone is supposed to grow and *gain* energy instead of losing it. Did I tell you that starfish are always growing? That's what you have to do to be a star."

"Always growing, yes. But how does that help us solve our problems this month?"

"People only do their best when they have opportunities to grow. As a manager, you need to use the latest crisis to help strengthen your people. If you achieve nothing else, you will at least be able to say that all of you are *stronger* as a result of your experiences."

"But . . . Oh, never mind. I believe you! How do I do it?"

"In the ocean, we sea people take our sports seriously. We play flukeball and reef hockey and lots of other games. I know you humans play sports too, because our favorite game, gulf, is like your golf—except at ninety fathoms down."

The manager looked at her blankly. *Gulf?*

"Don't you like sports?" the mermaid asked.

"Oh sure," the manager replied. "I like lots of sports."

"Then tell me, how do you help athletes improve their performance and become stronger players?"

"Well, let's see." He took a deep breath, thinking. "I guess you give them lots of chances to work out and practice. That and good advice and support when they need it. Right?"

"Exactly! And the key to making sure they have good opportunities to practice and increase their skills and strength is . . ." She waited for him to fill in the blank.

"Ah . . ." The answer seemed at least ninety fathoms down. "I really don't know, but I'd say that—"

"If you don't know, then why say anything?" the mermaid asked him. "I've noticed that you human managers often answer a question even when you're pretty sure you don't know the answer. Doesn't that ever get you in trouble?"

"I'm not sure," the manager joked, "so I'd rather not answer." Quickly realizing that he was the only one laughing, he added, "Okay, then. You tell me. How do you make sure an employee or an athlete is getting good opportunities to grow and develop?"

"The trick is to offer them *the* right *opportunities*," the mermaid answered. "Every employee should be doing things that require them to stretch a bit higher and lift a bit more weight than they did before. That's really all there is to it."

"So I just need to make sure everyone is challenged?" The manager's face brightened. "That's easy in our current situation! We all feel extremely challenged right now to solve our problems and help our unit survive."

"Is an extreme challenge the right opportunity for your employees from a growth perspective?" the mermaid asked. "I don't usually associate the word 'extreme' with the idea of a healthy challenge. Not unless people have been training and preparing and building up to it. You need to make sure your people have the *right* level of challenge for them at all times—not too little, but not too much either. Look at it this way. If you are used to bench-pressing 150 pounds, and you suddenly decide to lift 300 pounds instead, is that healthy? Are you going to succeed and get stronger, or just pull a muscle and hurt yourself?"

"Well, if I could switch from lifting weights up here to doing it under the water . . ." the manager said. "But no, I see your point, and it's possible that some of my employees are feeling overburdened by the challenges of our current crisis. On the other hand, maybe they were *under*-burdened before, when we didn't have a crisis, so they aren't in very good shape yet. How can I make sure they don't overdo it?"

"Do you know how much weight each of them can lift?"

"Ah, no, but I'd say . . . Actually, I won't say, since I really have no idea."

The mermaid laughed. "You're a quick learner, that's for sure! And you're right. In general, it's very hard for managers to know whether their employees are getting the right level of challenge and good opportunities for growth or not. So the obvious thing to do is to ask the employees themselves."

"You want me to ask them how hard they should be working?" The manager frowned in disbelief. "What if they all say they are working too hard and want to be given a break? Then where will we be?"

"You'd be face to face with their honest feelings at least!" the mermaid said. "You can't avoid asking important questions simply because you're afraid of the answers. Besides, I bet you're creative enough to come up with solutions that get the work done while also helping employees handle the strain. For instance, instead of giving them less work or easier challenges, maybe you just need to give them more support or help or advice or training to make their new loads more bearable. The athlete who can only lift 150 pounds on her own can easily lift 300 pounds if given access to a rope and pulley, right?"

Later on, in his hotel room, the manager reflected on the mermaid's advice and made the following list:

 BEACHCOMBERS INN

How to Provide *Developmental* Work and Supervise Challenges and Opportunities

✓ Ask what each person's interests and aspirations are.

✓ Give people stretch goals that require them to grow.

✓ Don't let people get overloaded. Pace and support their growth.

The manager had to think hard about that advice when he got back to the office and found Juanita waiting for him. She was not smiling.

The bad news was that one of the employees who had volunteered to lead a turnaround team didn't want to do it anymore and was asking to be replaced. Juanita was concerned because she couldn't find anyone else to lead the team.

Remembering the mermaid's advice, the manager wondered if the employee's problem was too much challenge all at once. He asked Juanita if he could speak to the employee, only to learn that she had called in sick the last two days because of a migraine headache.

"Do you think she is suffering from stress?" the manager asked anxiously.

"Who of us isn't?" Juanita said, shaking her head. "But I'd be surprised if Gloria was. She's always been such a steady worker."

The manager found this reassuring at first, but then remembered the mermaid's suggestion to ask the employee *personally* to find out whether he or she has the right level of challenge or not. Wanting to take no chances, he tracked down Gloria's phone number and gave her a call.

"Sorry to bother you when you aren't feeling well," he apologized. "This can wait until you get back if you prefer, but I hoped to speak with you about the new team project and see if there's anything I can do to help with it. I'm kind of concerned that you may feel you've had too much thrown on your shoulders all at once. Is that possible?"

There was a long pause on the other end of the phone, and the manager had to remind himself to be patient and not break the silence. Finally, he heard Gloria's voice. She confessed that, yes, to be honest, the project seemed like a much bigger burden than she'd expected when she volunteered. And now she had to make decisions about some technical questions that were way out of her field. On top of that, there were disagreements within the team and people weren't getting along very well, so it was getting more and more difficult to keep the meetings productive.

The manager grinned as he replied, "That's wonderful news, Gloria! I'm so glad to hear it!"

"You are? It sounds like pretty awful news to me," she said, obviously puzzled by his response.

"Oh, I know the problems are difficult," he assured her. "That's not why I'm happy. What I'm pleased about is that I now know what problems you are facing, and I think it should be fairly easy to help you out with them. Before, I had no idea what a mess you were dealing with, so you were on your own. Now I can help out."

"But what can you do?" Gloria asked, surprised.

"I don't know, but we can discuss it when you get back to the office. Maybe I can help you find someone who has the technical skills your team needs. There are some good people in our unit, but they aren't in your department, so you and Juanita wouldn't necessarily have access to them without my help. And if they can't solve your problems, we still have a little money in the budget for hiring consultants. Does that sound good?"

"It sounds great," Gloria said. "I'm sure we could make some progress if we had the right technical support."

"As for your people problems," the manager went on, "some of the conflict and negativity may evaporate if you get enough technical support. Your team members are probably feeling out of their depth on this project too. But if you continue to have attitude issues, I just happen to have a very good teacher who has been helping me with mine. I can share everything she's taught me, or maybe even set up a meeting with her if need be. Would you like that?"

"I guess so," she said, sounding a bit uncertain.

The manager was about to forge ahead with more advice when the question mark on his clam shell caught his eye. Quickly revising his approach, he said, "Can I ask you another question, Gloria?" When she consented, he continued, "Is running this team a challenge you could enjoy? Will it help you grow and develop? I was just wondering about your own goals and whether this might fit in."

"Gee!" Gloria said, taken by surprise. "Nobody has asked me what I want from my job for a long, long time. Not since I interviewed for it two years ago. Let me think . . . Well, what I'd like to do in the future is move on to some sort of management role in the company— or somewhere else if that becomes necessary. So I guess leading a team makes sense from that perspective, doesn't it?"

"Definitely," the manager agreed. "And all the more reason for you to handle the people issues yourself—with the help of that friend of mine I told you about, of course."

"Wow! I suddenly realized I'm feeling a lot better," Gloria said excitedly. "I may be able to come in after lunch. Do you think you might have time to meet with me today?"

"Absolutely," the manager said. "And I'd like to include Juanita too, if it's okay with you."

"Sure!" Gloria replied. "Juanita's cool! See you later."

The manager hung up the phone with a smile. He wondered briefly what made Juanita 'cool,' then remembered how often he'd seen her giving friendly advice and stopping to chat with other employees. Maybe some day they'd be saying he was cool too, he thought with a chuckle. But he was old enough not to really care about that. All he truly wanted was for the younger employees to think that his unit was a cool place to *work*. That was the key to getting their full involvement and support. And he was a lot closer to achieving that goal than he had ever been before.

Too bad he was also a lot closer to having the rug pulled out from under him than he had ever been before. The manager sighed. "Well," he told himself, "there's no point in getting discouraged. Maybe it's time to stop and take a look at our progress to date. I think we all need some 'up exercise' around now. And people have been doing some amazing things. In truth, there is a lot to celebrate."

7. The Progress Report

Т he manager looked around the conference room with pride. Team after team was reporting progress, and each report was greeted with clapping and congratulations. Costs were down significantly, productivity was up without the help of any temps, and overtime and sick time were down. His people were definitely proving they could deliver. The unit had never looked so good.

But a full month had gone by since he'd received the warning memo from headquarters, and there had been no further news. The manager felt a growing anxiety about what the company might be thinking and whether someone in the executive suite would pull the plug on his unit before they could complete the quarter and post their improved results. He wondered what their next move should be and whether they needed to improve their results even further.

So far, his efforts to discuss the situation with his boss had not been a success. First the man was travelling, then on vacation, and when he had finally replied, it was nothing more than a brief e-mail saying he couldn't go into it right now, but the manager would probably hear something about the fate of his unit by the end of the year. That was so vague, it left him feeling even more uncertain of their position.

He realized that everyone was staring at him.

"Did someone ask me a question?" he said. "I'm sorry, I was thinking."

"I asked you what our goals should be for cost savings and productivity improvements for the next month," Juanita said. "Just how far do we need to take this initiative in order to save our unit?"

"That's a very good question," the manager began. "While I don't have any exact data at this time, I'd say that—"

He stopped himself and took a deep breath, remembering the mermaid's advice not to speak when you don't know the answer.

"Actually, I'd be a fool to say anything because I simply have no idea," he corrected himself. "I haven't been able to talk to headquarters about it yet. But I'll try to find out what's going on, and report back to you next week if I possibly can. By the way, from your perspective working on these projects, can you tell me how much further you think it might be *possible* to go? Are this month's numbers pretty much the maximum we can do, or do you think there are more improvements in the pipeline?"

Juanita thought for a moment, then said, "My sense is that we've 'cherry-picked' some of the easiest improvements so far, and that it's probably going to get harder to keep improving the numbers. On the other hand, the work we've done so far has taught us a lot, and I think it's energized us. My hunch is that we could go quite a bit further if we really had to. But it might take a couple more months to move as far again as we've come in this first month."

There was general agreement with Juanita's assessment of the situation, and the manager left the meeting pleased with his group's growing confidence and competence. "It's great to know we can continue to find improvements," he thought. "But then again, I don't really know how far we have to go to stem the tide and impress headquarters favorably. They might just assume this month's results are a fluke and ignore them, for all I know. I just don't know what the best move is at this point. I think I need some advice on what to do next. Maybe I ought to see if I can find the mermaid and run this by her."

It was a long drive to the coast, but the manager had discovered a couple of short cuts that shaved a half hour off the trip. And he'd learned that by leaving after rush hour, he could save another half hour at least. So he made record time to the Beachcombers Inn that evening, where he presented himself at the desk and apologized for not having called in earlier to reserve a room.

"Oh, it's you again," the night clerk said. "You're the only guest we have who only comes on weekdays. What the heck do you do here anyway? You always seem to be dressed for work."

"I *am* working," the manager assured the clerk, who gave him a suspicious look—but also the key to a room and a discount too because he was such a regular visitor.

The manager tossed his overnight bag on the bed, got a diet cola from the vending machine at the end of the hall, and walked out into the darkness to find his way to the beach.

He was a day early for his next rendezvous with the mermaid, but he sensed he needed to do some thinking in a hurry and hoped she would be at her regular spot—the place where the surf was highest.

8. A Light in the Dark

The manager recalled something he'd heard someone say a long time ago: "When you are ready, the teacher will appear." He hoped it was true, because he sure could use a little more advice. And yet he realized he had no way of contacting the mermaid to let her know in advance that he had decided to come to the ocean that night. And so far, no teacher had appeared. He sure needed one about now—but he had to admit he wasn't sure that needing help and being "ready" for it were quite the same thing.

He sat on the rock in the dark for a long time, wondering how to call a mermaid. He really had no idea, but so far she seemed to have an uncanny ability to appear at the right moment. He hoped that she would do her magical appearing act again tonight.

An hour later, the manager was feeling rather discouraged. He had grown tired of sitting on the rock and had moved down the beach to a spot where he could sit on the sand and watch the waves roll in. But it was too dark to see very much, and he was getting bored.

Finally he chuckled to himself and said, "What am I doing sitting out here in the dark waiting for a mermaid to rescue me! If she's not around, then I might as well try to rescue myself. I ought to show a little of the same initiative I value so much in my employees."

So he decided he would take advantage of the nice night and the soft murmur of waves to walk along the beach and try to clear his head. Maybe he would come up with an insight of his own. Things were, he reflected, a great deal better than they had been the first time he came to this beach and sat on the rock feeling helpless. At least now he had an enthusiastic group and a workplace in which everyone was trying their best.

It was truly a high-performance work environment now. It just lacked *focus*, that's all. If he only knew what headquarters was thinking or how the economic trends were going to go, he'd be better able to guide his unit, he thought. But right now, he realized as he strolled down the inky beach with his hands in his pockets, right now he just wasn't sure *where* exactly they were going or what it would take to secure their future.

"Ouch!" he cried out as he stumbled over a low rock, banging his shins painfully. "Chri . . . I mean sh . . . I mean *darn* it! I can't see a *thing* out here!"

Then he laughed at his own foolishness for thinking he could walk the beach on a night as black as this one. He carefully picked his way back to the hotel parking lot, unlocked the trunk of his car, and extracted the flashlight he kept there for emergencies. "I guess this *is* an emergency," he thought, "because if I don't figure out where we need to go, we certainly won't get there. And if I don't walk on the beach, I'll just sit in my hotel room watching reruns, and then I *definitely* won't come up with any insights into where we need to go!"

It proved a pleasant night for a seaside stroll now that he could see where he was going. The sky was dark—too cloudy for the stars to show—but the air was warm and still, and there was a pleasant scent of salt and sand. The rhythmic rumble of the waves relaxed him, and soon he had walked to the end of the long beach and started to climb along the rocky stretch where the mermaid had shown him the tide pools. Now the tide was in, though, and there were no pools to be seen.

He shone his flashlight into the water and leaned over to peer at a submerged rock. A few feet down, clinging to the rocks, was a starfish. It began to move gracefully over the stone as if it knew just where it wanted to go.

"I wish *I* knew where we were going," the manager muttered.

"Did I hear someone make a wish?" a cheerful voice asked from the darkness.

"Is that you?" the manager cried happily. "I was hoping I'd find you here tonight!"

"All you have to do is make a wish and I'll appear," the mermaid explained. "Say, that's a nice light you've got there. Must make it easier to walk in the dark."

"Yes," the manager confirmed. "And I guess that's kind of what my wish is about too. You see, now we have a much more positive and energetic workplace, and everyone is eager to turn things around and solve our problems. But we aren't quite sure what to do next. I think we are working too much in the dark. We need to know what lies ahead. Can you tell me what exactly we need to do to assure our survival?"

The mermaid laughed. "You want me to be your flashlight?" she kidded him. "Sorry, but that's more than even I can do. I can't tell you what the future holds. I'm afraid there is no such thing as a certainty in the world of leadership. You always have to accept that the future may hold surprises or work out differently from how you expect."

"You mean you can't help me?" he said in a disappointed tone of voice. "But I thought . . ."

"You thought I could work magic for you?" she said. "I told you at the beginning that I can't grant your wishes through magic. I can only give you good advice."

"Well, do you have any good advice for me now?" the manager asked.

"Of course!" the mermaid replied. "I wanted to tell you something else anyway, and I think it's just what you need right now. You have gone as far as you can with my earlier advice, and now you are ready for the next lesson. But first, do you remember everything I told you before?"

"Sure," the manager said, since he had just been sharing the lessons with Gloria and Juanita in his meeting with them. "We have been working on making our workplace more considerate, positive, creative, informed, and, and . . ." His mind drew a blank. He realized just how tired he was after the full day of work and the long drive to the coast. "Maybe that's all," he said uncertainly. "I can't remember if there were four or five lessons."

"To make sure *I* don't forget," the mermaid told him, "I always think of the starfish. It has five arms—one for each of the lessons I've taught you so far."

"Strengthening!" the manager interrupted. "That's the fifth lesson, and we've been working on it by helping each employee find the right level of challenge and the right opportunities for growth."

"Good!" the mermaid said enthusiastically. "Now can you guess what's left?"

"After those five? Hmm. The starfish only has five arms, so what else could there be?"

"Why don't you take a good, hard look at a starfish," the mermaid suggested, "and tell me what else you see."

The manager used his flashlight to find the starfish again. It had moved several feet, so it took him a minute to find it. He looked at it carefully and counted the arms. There were definitely only five of them, and he couldn't see any other distinguishing features. The creature seemed to be almost all arms.

"I'm not sure," he said. "Got any hints for me?"

"If you were going to describe a starfish to someone who'd never seen one, how would you do it?" the mermaid prompted.

"Well, it's like a star, with five long arms around a small central body. That's about it."

"Is it?" the mermaid asked.

The manager took another look at the starfish.

"That's about all there is to it," he said, "except for that little gold bump near the middle."

"And what do you think that is?" the mermaid asked.

"I don't know. An eye maybe. Yes, it must be the creature's eye. I never realized they had eyes before."

"Of course it has an eye!" the mermaid said. "How else could it see where it's going? And as a manager, you have to make sure your people can see where they are going too. Even if it's dark and the visibility isn't very good, you have to serve as their eye and give them a clear destination to pursue."

"So the eye represents the sixth lesson?" the manager guessed.

"Exactly! It reminds us that a healthy, energized workplace needs to be *directional*. The people in it have to have a shared vision of their destination. They need to use their energy and enthusiasm to *go* somewhere. And your job as a manager is to make sure they have a good destination clearly in view."

"But I can't be sure what's going to happen," the manager complained. "I don't really—"

"Are you still using 'but' in your talk?" the mermaid scolded.

"I'm comfortable now with the other lessons, and I see how to apply them," the manager explained. "But I don't really see how I can make the workplace more directional. That seems difficult. There isn't an obvious, clear destination right now."

"If there were, why would your people need a leader?" the mermaid asked pointedly. "This is where you get to add some extra value. While they are busy dealing with all the daily challenges of their jobs, you need to spend some time looking around and deciding where to go next."

"But I . . . Yes, you're right," the manager agreed reluctantly. "It's just that it is so hard to know where we're going or what the future holds . . ."

"Is it *completely* dark?"

"Well, no, not completely. I guess I can see a little way into the future, but not very far. For instance, I can see that the company is likely to shut our unit down, but that if we manage to improve our performance significantly, they're not as likely to do so. I just don't know exactly how well we'd have to perform to ensure that we never get shut down."

"Three things," the mermaid said. "First, can you improve your certainty at all? Because if so, then you might as well do it before you decide what goals to shoot for. No point making a decision until you have as much information as you can. And second, do you have to have 100 percent certainty before making a decision? Because if so, then you might as well give it up now. Nobody gets to make leadership decisions with absolute certainty. There is always some risk and guesswork in it. You simply have to do the best you can with the cards you get dealt."

"Do you play cards?" the manager asked, trying to picture mermaids playing poker underwater.

"Shall we stick to the point?" the mermaid said.

"Oh, sorry. Okay, where were we . . . Can I improve my certainty before deciding what our destination should be? Well, I guess so, if I can just talk to headquarters and run some scenarios by them. I get the feeling they're ducking my calls because they figure I'll try to talk them out of closing us down."

"I see," said the mermaid. "So naturally you've done everything you can to get a meeting set up to discuss it?"

"Everything I can? Um, well, I've called a couple of times and sent a few e-mails, but I haven't gotten a definite response yet. It's only been a few weeks, really, and of course this is the time of year when most executives take their vacations."

The mermaid sighed. "Remind me of all those qualities you said you wanted your people to have. Like persistence and initiative and optimism. I believe you also mentioned creative problem-solving, and—"

"Okay, okay!" the manager cried. "I get the point! I could certainly be more persistent in trying to nail my management down and get some clearer information, if not a definite commitment. I'll see what I can do. I guess I could just send an e-mail to my boss saying I'm on my way, then drive to headquarters to see him. I don't see how he could avoid meeting me under those circumstances. I could check with his secretary first to make sure it was a day when he was supposed to be in."

"Good thinking!" the mermaid complimented him. "And then what?"

"Well, I could show him our progress so far, and explain that we are determined to show how well our unit is capable of performing and that we can be profitable for the company. Then I could propose that he let us stay open if we achieve certain performance levels throughout the coming year. I can work out pretty well what numbers we'd have to reach to contribute positively to the bottom line. He might not be willing to make a long-term commitment, but he might at least go for a one-year guarantee as long as we can make the numbers work for him. I guess then we could go back and try to negotiate for another year or two if we manage to meet our targets in the first year. Do you think that sounds reasonable?"

"You're asking the wrong person," the mermaid told him, "but it does sound good to me. How soon do you think you can get to your company's headquarters and run it by your boss?"

"If I drive back to my office tomorrow morning, send him a message, then pack up and head out, I guess I could get there tomorrow night, stay at a hotel or something, and see him the next morning."

"Headquarters sounds far away. Too bad you have to do so much driving. It's not on the ocean, is it? Maybe you could swim."

"Uh, I don't swim very fast," the manager laughed. "But now that you mention it, headquarters is a lot closer to this place than it is to my office. Maybe I'll just drive straight there tomorrow morning and surprise him."

"I bet you'll make a real splash," the mermaid said.

"Okay, I better be going!" The manager enthusiastically turned to leave. "See you later!"

"Aren't you going to ask me what the third thing is?" the mermaid said, laughing at his excitement.

The manager turned back, puzzled. "Third thing? I don't remember a third thing. What is it?"

"Of course you don't remember. I haven't told you about it yet. The third thing is simply this: that by *acting*, by taking initiative, you reduce the uncertainty of the future. Do you know why?"

"Um, no."

"Because you help *create* the future. The leader who has a clear enough vision of where to go and is courageous enough to pursue it, tends to shape the future instead of being a victim of it."

"Ah, I see what you mean," the manager said. "If I wait around for headquarters to decide what to do about us, I have no control over our fate. But if I take the initiative, I may be able to make the decision for them. For example, let's say our plant is so successful, they can't ignore it; then they really wouldn't have the option of shutting us down, would they? So instead of worrying about the future, maybe we should decide to do our utmost best to become the ones in charge of it."

"Now you're thinking like a real leader!" the mermaid said. "And with the work you've done to create a positive climate for work, your employees are ready to create that future with you. I don't think you're going to need my help now. Goodbye, and good luck!"

"Hey, when will I see you—"

But the mermaid had disappeared.

The manager suddenly felt an overwhelming sense of gratitude. "Goodnight, my friend! Thanks for all the help!" he shouted into the darkness of the sea.

 BEACHCOMBERS INN

How to Provide *Directional* Work

Supervise WHY people work,
not just what they do:

✓   Develop an energizing view of the destination.

✓   Share your view of the destination with those who are essential to getting there.

✓   Question any work that is not relevant to the journey.

✓   Celebrate progress on the journey.

9. Flexibility

The manager did meet with his boss, who was so impressed by the unit's recent performance figures that he called in the chief executive to look at them too. They praised the manager's efforts and told him that if he kept up the good work, he'd go far—although they weren't very specific about which direction he'd go far in, and whether it would be with that company or not!

Nor were they willing to give him a firm guarantee that his unit would be kept open. They explained that the board was going to consider whether to close all the units at their next meeting, in two week's time. But the good news was that they *did* promise to share his unit's remarkable results with the board as an example of what might be possible. And that, the manager thought, was probably the best he could have expected from them in the company's current condition.

As it turned out, the board was pleasantly surprised by the report on the unit and its dramatic progress. Instead of shutting his unit down, the board voted to give the manager another year to show what he could do.

In fact, they voted to keep *all* the facilities in their division open for another year, and told the company to roll out the manager's new methods to the other units as well. This caused some consternation at headquarters, since nobody there had any idea how his team had done it.

Suddenly, his vice president was not only returning his calls, but calling up regularly to ask for advice. There was still no guarantee, but things were looking a lot better now for the manager and his crew.

The manager shared all this good news with his people, and they decided to try for even better numbers in the coming year. In fact, they adopted a set of targets that would produce a truly remarkable year . . . *if* they were able to achieve them. This was their chance to create the future—a future that involved their continued success.

This, the manager realized, was not just the successful end of his quest to motivate his group and build a high-performing team. It was also the beginning of a new journey, one that would require them all to work very hard and achieve significant breakthroughs in the coming year. Now they had a real opportunity to prove themselves, and they had a wonderful sense of enthusiasm and confidence in their team. But, to be honest, they also had an uphill fight ahead. Their initial results were impressive but still short of the goal, and the next steps were going to be more complicated than the easy ones his group had tackled first.

Unfortunately, his people also were, in a sense, victims of their own success. Headquarters was so impressed by their progress that it asked the manager to send some of his best employees to other units in order to spread their new ideas and cost-saving methods throughout the company.

The manager had come to trust Gloria and Juanita more and more, as they had developed into real leaders and delivered increasingly good results. Now he realized he had also become dependent on them, and didn't have a clear plan for what to do once they were gone.

Soon Gloria was promoted to assistant manager of another unit, a personal goal fulfilled. (The manager gave her a farewell gift of a brass plaque with a starfish etched into it, to help her remember how to use the mermaid's lessons in her new job.) When shortly thereafter Juanita was moved away to supervise another unit, the manager got down to the difficult task of finding replacements for them both.

His hopes turned to Dave and Annie, two more employees who had been eager contributors to the effort so far. Dave was fairly new, but he had worked with Gloria for a couple of months. Annie had been one of Juanita's best employees. The manager explained to them that promotion would mean their stepping into the shoes of their previous bosses and keeping up the momentum. Neither was daunted by the challenge. They were both excited to be promoted, and jumped right in with enthusiasm.

The manager was pleased to have filled these two positions, especially because he had a business trip in the coming week. Before he left, he told Dave and Annie that he had faith in their skill and judgment, and put them in charge of the next staff meeting and the initial discussions of how to implement the new plans. "What a relief," he thought, "to be able to trust everyone to take initiative and stay focused and motivated when I'm gone!"

Although he didn't know it, that was the moment when things began to unravel again.

When he got back to the office the following Monday, he found a white envelope addressed to him and placed prominently on his desktop. Inside was a formal resignation letter from Dave, stating that he was giving two week's notice.

The manager immediately called Dave into his office.

"You can't leave now," the manager protested, fighting his own panic. "I'm counting on you to help me lead our unit through the coming year. Besides, you were so enthusiastic just a week ago. What in the world could have happened to make you change your mind?"

Dave sighed and rubbed his forehead as if the memory hurt. "I don't think I'm cut out for management," he confessed with a shudder. "Everybody liked me before, but now they all seem to hate me and won't do what I tell them to do. You should have seen the staff meeting last week—it was a disaster! I tried to give out team assignments and improvement targets, but everyone argued with me, and in the end, they all refused to accept their assignments. Since then, most of them have been avoiding me and not replying to my e-mails."

"Ah," the manager said, now smiling. "Sometimes leadership isn't as simple as just telling people what to do. Maybe I should have given you a bit more help before I tossed you into the deep end. Will you let me think about this for a little while and see if I can come up with a solution?"

Dave agreed to wait on his decision about whether to quit, and he and the manager scheduled a long meeting for the next day. "I promise I'll have something helpful by then," the manager said. "I'm going to start working on it right now."

Before he could get settled into the task, though, he was interrupted by a delegation of five employees who insisted they had an emergency on their hands.

It turned out that their "emergency" was his other newly promoted leader, Annie, who, they said, was changing everything and causing all sorts of problems. "She's not at all like Juanita," they complained. "She doesn't know what she's talking about, and keeps getting in our way. We're not doing anything until you get rid of her!"

Once the manager had ushered them out of his office, promising again to think about the situation and come up with a solution, he called Annie and asked her to meet with him the following day too. Now he had *two* major personnel problems to deal with, and less than 24 hours to figure out what to do. If only he had time to return to the beach and talk to the mermaid—but he wasn't even sure if she would be there.

Then the manager remembered the e-mail that she had sent him so long ago. Would such a strange thing still be in his message log? If so, perhaps he could contact her through a reply. He set to work, scrolling through months of messages, and was pleased to find that, sure enough, the e-mail was still there. However, the cryptic nature of the sender's address had somehow simplified itself to "leaderhelp@fluke.atlantis."

"Why does anything surprise me anymore?" the manager asked himself with a shake of the head.

He carefully summarized the problems with his newly promoted people, pressed "Send," and sat back to see what would happen. Before long, his computer's screen-saver clicked on. He watched it idly, somehow enjoying its presence more and more. In fact, the manager realized, he was enjoying its presence *too* much. He sat bolt-straight and stared at the screen. This was not the screen-saver he usually saw.

It seemed he was looking through a window into the sea. A beautiful coral reef was there, with colorful fish darting to and fro. And now, crawling across the reef, was a large starfish. As it moved over the coral and rocks, it flexed and bent in an impressively supple manner. "It really is *remarkably* flexible," the manager thought. Why hadn't he noticed this about starfish before?

"Yes, it *is* quite flexible, isn't it?" a familiar voice asked through the swishing, watery sounds rising from his computer. The mermaid's face floated into view. "And you are, I see, ready for the seventh and final lesson the starfish has to teach you. For you have made the classic leadership error of treating all your employees the same way instead of being flexible for them."

"Hi!" the manager happily greeted her. "How are you doing? It's nice to see you again."

"Are you changing the subject," the mermaid said, "or can I continue to discuss your error?"

"Well, no, I want to hear what you have to say, that's why I contacted you," the manager replied. "But I wasn't so much thinking about my own performance as the performances of my two new supervisors. I mean, it seems to me that they are the ones who have been making errors while I've been gone. I never had to worry about Gloria or Juanita messing things up in my absence like they did."

"As you are their leader, their errors are your errors," the mermaid pointed out. "It's much more useful to think about what *you* could do different and better, instead of blaming *them*. After all, it's relatively simple for you to change your own approach. And speaking of that, do you know what approach you have been using with these two employees so far?"

"Well, I've tried to trust them and give them the same responsibilities that Juanita and Gloria had, and—"

"Yes, exactly," the mermaid interrupted. "But is that a good strategy? They don't have Gloria or Juanita's experience yet. If you'll recall, you didn't give Gloria or Juanita that much responsibility a year ago. So while you certainly want to trust your new supervisors, you *don't* want to trust them at the same level as their predecessors. Your approach so far has been to delegate to them—which means you told them to take charge and gave them plenty of opportunity to succeed or fail on their own. And guess what? Whenever you do that before a person is ready, that person will fail rather than succeed. Guaranteed."

"I guess that makes sense," the manager said. "And I don't want to set people up for failure. So what approach would you suggest?"

"I'm going to give you some information, then let you answer that question for yourself."

The screen turned blurry, then sharpened into the image of a graph floating against a wavy blue background. There were four cells to the graph, each one labeled with the name of a leadership approach. The graph's axes were labeled too. (This is illustrated in Figure 1.)

If employee has:	Strategic Leadership Grid	
Low Enthusiasm	**Relate**	**Coach**
High Enthusiasm	**Delegate**	**Instruct**

If employee has:

High Capability   Low Capability

Figure 1

"But I don't see what I did wrong," the manager said as he looked at the diagram. "My employees started out with lots of enthusiasm when I promoted them. They just seem to have lost their positive attitudes while I was gone."

"NO MORE 'BUTS'!" the mermaid said rather sternly. "Now, I want you to read that graph more carefully instead of being defensive. Notice that to delegate, you need employees who have both high enthusiasm and high capabilities. Your two newly promoted people clearly lack the management skills of their more experienced predecessors, so what approach should you have used instead of delegating?"

"I should have instructed them, right? Does that mean I needed to tell them more specifically what to do, instead of simply assuming they would figure it out?"

"*Exactly!*" the mermaid cried out in high praise. "You could have given them specific instructions, yes. Or you could have arranged for Juanita and Gloria to mentor them from a distance—then they could have asked 'the experts' questions and gotten some tips before taking action. There are plenty of ways to be more instructive as a leader than you were—it's just a matter of realizing when you need to use those ways. In fact, I'd recommend you meet with Dave and Annie for a little while each day for the next few weeks, to discuss their efforts and give them tips and instructions. It can take some time to acquire the skills to manage well, especially in a high-performance workplace where there are major leadership challenges."

"Good idea!" the manager said enthusiastically. "I guess I tend to be a 'sink or swim'–style manager, but I can be flexible and adjust my leadership strategy when my employees need me to do that. I'll be more instructive with Dave and Annie from now on, at least until they're ready for me to delegate to them."

"Not so fast!" the mermaid warned with a laugh. "We were talking about what you should have done a week ago, when your newly promoted supervisors were still enthusiastic. But now they've been getting lots of negative results for a whole week, and their attitudes have deteriorated. Where would you say they are now on that grid?"

"Oh dear, I see what you mean. Let's see . . . Low enthusiasm is on this row, and low capability in this column. That adds up to a need for coaching, right?"

"Exactly," the mermaid confirmed. "And that means you need to work on their attitudes and their skills by helping them achieve some step-by-step successes. In fact, you had better start with their attitudes, because nobody is very open to learning if they are down and discouraged. What can you do to help them not only regain some enthusiasm but also do the right things and learn their new jobs?"

"Wow, this being flexible isn't as easy as it sounds! I'm going to have to clear my calendar this week and focus on coaching my two new supervisors, aren't I? Hmm . . . Maybe I ought to take them out to lunch at a nice restaurant tomorrow, and spend some time encouraging them and reminding them of all the great things they've done in the past. *Then* I can try to tell them what to do next. After that, I can—"

"You're on the right course," the mermaid broke in. "It may sound like a lot of work, but remember: if you put the effort into coaching them now, you will reap the rewards of having employees whom you really can delegate to later."

"One more thing," the manager said. "What's the fourth approach, where it says to 'relate' to employees?"

"Do you remember the very first lessons I gave you?"

"Yes, they were to be considerate and positive, correct? And to do people work before paperwork."

"Right, and that means focusing on supporting and encouraging the person, *instead of* focusing on getting the work done. Sometimes focusing only on people and their needs is the right thing to do, especially when morale is low. You made great progress last summer, and you did it by building and maintaining high morale. If some of your employees grow discouraged and their morale slips, they won't continue to perform well, *even if they know how*. In that case, you don't want to focus on the work and how to do it; you want to focus on the people and help them feel better about their work."

"Okay, I accept that strategy in principle," the manager said. "But it must be an uncommon situation, right?"

"Not as uncommon as you might think!" the mermaid replied. "In fact, more employees are performing below their potential because of attitude or morale problems than because of lack of skill or capability. Can you think of any examples in your organization?"

"Certainly not!" the manager said defensively. "We have a good overall level of morale right now."

"Except for all those employees who are resentful of their new supervisors and complaining about them."

"Ah . . . that's true. Except for them," he admitted. "I'd forgotten about Dave's employees, and the ones who came in earlier, complaining about Annie. Actually, those people know perfectly well what to do—they just don't want to do it because of how they think they're being treated. Do you suggest I use the Relate strategy with them?"

"*Someone* needs to do it," the mermaid told him. "But perhaps it should be their own supervisor. Let's start with Annie. Wouldn't that be a good first project to coach her through? If you help her turn around people's attitudes, and *make sure she succeeds,* she'll gain a lot of confidence and skills. And her employees will gain a lot of respect for their new supervisor. But remember, the coach's role must be to help stretch employees with challenges that they can succeed at. You don't want to set anyone up to fail, okay?"

"Sure. And I think I know where to suggest that Annie start. If I were in her situation—and I used to get into situations like this all the time—I'd begin with an honest apology. Then I'd do something simple to show that I care and want to patch things up. Yes, I think that's a good focus for Annie and me to work on tomorrow.

"Now, let's see. What should I do about Dave? I think his main issue right now is not asking for enough participation. He's probably afraid of losing control if he does—I remember feeling that way. But if he . . ."

The manager started to take notes, continuing to mutter to himself as he planned the next day's meetings. He didn't notice it when his normal screen-saver came back on and the sounds of swishing water stopped. When he next looked up, the mermaid was gone and his office had returned to normal.

"Darn it," he said to himself. "I wanted to say goodbye and this time thank her properly for all her help. Oh well, I guess it's never really goodbye. She seems to pop up whenever she's most needed. I hope I'll get a chance to talk to her again . . . or maybe I don't, because that will mean I have another problem I can't solve! Well, I'll just have to see what the future brings. But in the meantime, I can't wait to put these ideas to use and help Annie and Dave learn how to fill Juanita and Gloria's shoes."

10. Afloat Again

In a few weeks, the new supervisors improved and the manager was able to reduce his daily meetings with them to twice a week. By midway through the year, they were down to one meeting a week and Dave and Annie were handling the majority of their challenges without his help. But when they ran into an unfamiliar problem or got stuck, they would let the manager know and he would provide more assistance as needed.

The rest of the unit was growing and learning too as everyone struggled to cut costs, introduce helpful innovations, and overcome new problems. Morale stayed high throughout the winter and spring, and the manager made sure it did by using what he came to call his "smile test" on a regular basis. At least once a week, he or one of his supervisors would walk through the facilities, stopping briefly to chat with or simply observe people at work. They would also take special note of the mood.

Were people "up"—enthusiastic and motivated? Were they smiling while they worked? If not, the manager would revisit the lessons he'd learned from the mermaid and get to work on boosting morale again. It didn't happen very often now, but occasionally he or a supervisor would find that people were getting discouraged, in which case they'd switch to a focus on attitudes and feelings until it was "safe" to refocus on results.

Soon a year was almost past, and the manager was amazed by how much energy and enthusiasm there was in his workplace. It was a joy to come to work most days. Sure, there were still a few unpleasant surprises, and sometimes he still had to roll up his sleeves and put out a fire that he wished his employees had handled better on their own or simply had prevented. But most of the time, his people took the initiative to solve problems and achieve goals on their own. There were far fewer problems, and the results looked better and better because of everyone's continuing efforts. In fact, his unit was consistently the most profitable in his division and was leading the way toward unprecedented levels of achievement—the closest thing to a guarantee he realized he'd ever be able to get.

The future was still uncertain, the manager knew, but things now looked good enough that he was feeling optimistic about his unit's prospects. Headquarters was positive about their performance too, and the talk of closing them down had stopped.

But even if the worst were to happen and his unit had to close some day, at least now they were all a lot stronger and more able. Each and every one of them was a star. They would land on their feet, no matter what happened. No tide was going to leave any of *them* stranded!

To celebrate their success, the manager decided to throw a big party for his staff. Maybe they all could go somewhere special, he thought. Somewhere relaxing, where they could get away from their work and have some fun together. But *exactly* where?

"I've got it!" the manager exclaimed a split-second later. "I'll take them to the beach!" It now all seemed so obvious. "Maybe we can even rent the Beachcombers Inn for a weeknight at the end of the season. I'll have to give the place a call."

Did the mermaid show up for their celebration? Did they run into new challenges, and did they overcome them too? Where are they now? I wish I could answer these questions, but the Starfish Files end at this point, and we don't have any further information upon which to rely. Sure, there are the rumors, and some of them may be true. I've heard great things about the manager and his employees—how they all went on to success after success, and how they spread their new methods and skills with them in ever-expanding ripples as they took on new jobs and overcame new challenges in their careers.

These rumors no doubt have a grain of truth in them, but what we do know for sure is that the manager's remarkable year was made possible by a new lease on life and a willingness to reexamine his assumptions and his own contributions as a leader. And we know that he attributes his later success to these experiences, and to the rather remarkable teacher who first came to him in one of his blackest moments, while he was sitting alone on a long, windy beach, wondering how he would ever cope.

I think that if the mermaid were here to draw a lesson from the manager's experience, at the core of that lesson would be the simple observation that, no matter how bleak a situation may appear, there is *always* hope for those who are open to new ideas and approaches in their work as leaders.

End Note:
Becoming a Launcher of Stars

"I picked up a star whose tube feet ventured timidly among my fingers while, like a true star, it cried soundlessly for life. I saw it with an unaccustomed clarity and cast it far out."
—Loren C. Eiseley, from *The Star Thrower*

Since I first documented the experiences contained in *The Starfish Files,* a number of readers have asked me if the story was inspired by another, older story about starfish. I didn't know that story at the time, but I looked it up and it is worth recounting. The story is often told something as follows.

A man is walking down the beach one morning after a storm. The sea has cast flotsam high up the beach, and among the sea wrack there are hundreds and hundreds of starfish. Some have died, but some still have life in them. The man shakes his head, regretting the cruelty of nature, but keeps on walking, for there are so many starfish that he realizes it would be impossible to try to save them.

Then he sees a child ahead of him who is alternately stooping down and standing up, throwing things out to the sea. As the man draws even with the child, he sees that she is holding a single starfish in the palm of her hand.

"What are you doing?" he says. "Don't you realize that you can't possibly save them all? Even if you work all day at it, it won't really matter in the grand scheme of things."

Now, I imagine that this exchange might have happened at some point between the manager in *The Starfish Files* and his daughter (with whom he was on vacation when he first met his mentor). And what does the child say in this classic tale?

She replies, "How can you say my help doesn't matter? It matters to *this* starfish."

And of course, she is right: it does.

This story was experienced by the great naturalist Loren Eiseley, on a beach in Costabel, and you can find it in a collection of his works called *The Star Thrower* (Harcourt Brace, 1978). It is not told quite as I have heard it from word of mouth, and have told it here. But I expect the experience may be one that is played out in different ways between the old at heart and the young at heart across the beaches of the world on many occasions.

What does this story mean and why is it so widely retold, often by people who have never heard of Loren Eiseley? I think it symbolizes faith, life, humanity, and similar qualities that we most value in ourselves and others. And it shows how we can become jaded to the world as we struggle through our busy lives, and forget how simple it is to help another, to act in the faith that each generous-hearted action matters to someone and is thus very much worthwhile.

As the mermaid says in *The Starfish Files,* one drop at a time.

In leadership, there is often the presumption of power—power of position, power of resources at one's command. Yet in reality, the needs and purposes that concern a leader can seem daunting and vast, and many in a *position* to lead do not *choose* to do so as often as they might or could. They, like the weary, cynical man walking down the beach, may just plain feel that they cannot make enough of a difference for it to really matter.

At times like this, the story of the little girl (or any other starfish thrower) should come to mind. Each starfish saved makes a small ripple as its splashes back into its life-giving sea. Each act made in kindness, faith, or desire to bring about any positive change also makes a ripple, no matter how small that ripple may be. And anyone who chooses to throw stars, or to speak kind or encouraging words to others, or to articulate a vision of how a group might improve things or achieve a worthy goal, is creating the same ripple effect.

Where do those ripples go? Their progress may be hard to see, superimposed as it were on the often far larger waves of the vast oceans of our world, but those ripples *do* go forth, touch others, stimulate more ripples, and act as a powerful force for positive change—perhaps far more powerful than the initial star thrower, or good-deed doer, or caring leader, could ever have imagined. What goes around comes around, as the old saying so aptly puts it.

The manager in *The Starfish Files* learns this lesson for the first time when he is instructed to begin his journey by bringing back a small gift and a kind thought for those he is expected to lead. These small ripples begin a process of growth and change, not just for him, but for everyone he works with and, in the end, for everyone *they* work with. The ripples spread outward. And if each of us is willing to stoop, pick up a star (no matter how small), and toss it as far as our strength will permit, the ripples will go on forever.

—Alex Hiam, Amherst, MA

Appendix

Executive Summary of Key Learning Points in

The Starfish Files

I t may be more difficult than ever to be an effective leader. How can you overcome problems and threats, break through to higher performance levels, and generate enthusiasm and self-motivated initiative in employees who often feel at risk or stressed out themselves?

The core set of leadership skills taught in *The Starfish Files* focuses on special competencies needed to meet these challenges, including:

1. Creating a considerate workplace in which people take pride in treating one another with kindness and respect

2. Managing with "emotional intelligence" to maximize optimism and hopefulness in your group

3. Inviting more participative problem-solving and creative idea generation from your staff

4. Sharing the power of performance-related information with all of your people (who, in the typical workplace, have a dearth of useful feedback)

5. Bringing a strengthening, developmental element to your employees' assignments

6. Having the courage to be the "eyes" of your team, providing the compelling goal or direction that gives their work context and meaning

7. Recognizing that these practices create an overall climate for high performance, but may not meet the needs of every individual as unique challenges present themselves. As a leader, you need to assess the changing needs of individuals and *adjust your approach flexibly,* to help everyone develop and fulfill his or her unique "star" potential.

These practices are powerful and, once put on paper, can seem simple and intuitive. Yet they are *not used* very often by managers today.

Why don't we use these practices more often and fully? In part it is because these are *emerging* competencies and skills, ones that were not as relevant in a traditional top-down, command-and-control workplace as they are in the more flexible workplace of today. Also, these practices rely on good self-management of one's own internal emotional state or perspective, and of one's behavior toward others in the workplace.

Self-managing our attitudes and behaviors is a tough thing to do, and not an easy thing to teach or learn. Have you ever been out to dinner at a nice restaurant and had the waiter order you to "enjoy your meal" when serving the food? You know it's not that simple! The cooking better be good or it doesn't matter what the waiter says. And in management and executive leadership, you need to go deeper than good-sounding words of advice.

That's why this book uses a story and a leader's challenges to illustrate key principles of modern leadership. Try to incorporate these principles into your own "story" by letting them shape your actions and interactions in the coming days and weeks. You may be surprised how far a little effort on your part will go when it is amplified and reciprocated by your group!

The Starfish Reminds Us
Our Workplace Needs to Be More . . .

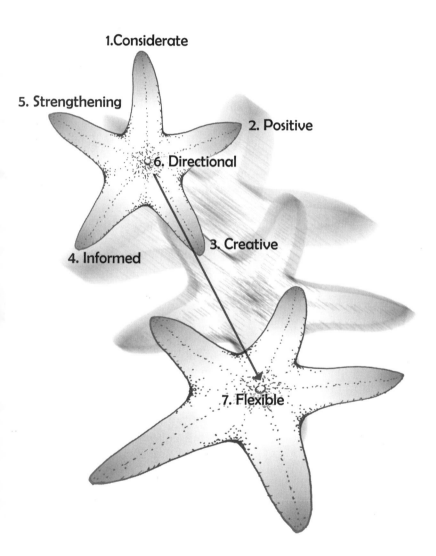

1. Considerate
5. Strengthening
2. Positive
6. Directional
3. Creative
4. Informed
7. Flexible

When leaders remember to focus on these areas,
they create a climate that maximizes success.

About the Author

Alex Hiam is the president of INSIGHTS for Training & Development, and is an enthusiastic teacher and student of business leadership—a subject he has addressed in his consulting, research, and writing for two decades. He began his work in leadership as an advisor to executives and boards in the '80s, both as a consultant and as a member of the strategic planning staff for Fortune 100 firms. He currently provides training for executives, supervisors, and managers in a wide variety of organizations, including small and large companies and government agencies. His first book to explore leadership and performance issues was *The Vest Pocket CEO: Decision-Making Tools for Executives* (Prentice Hall, 1990), in which he wrote about participatory decision-making, nonfinancial motivators, motivation of selling teams, and other foundational issues of modern business leadership.

In the early '90s, Hiam studied leadership and employee involvement issues in the quality improvement movement, performing case studies and surveys for a Conference Board report and (in his statistical studies) showing stronger links between leadership and profitability than previously reported. He also explored leadership in turnaround cases at top U.S. companies in his 1992 book, *Closing the Quality Gap* (written with The Conference Board for Prentice Hall).

In 1996, Hiam addressed leadership and management issues in new and high-growth firms in *The Entrepreneur's Complete Sourcebook* after consulting to many Silicon Valley management teams. In 1997 his *Portable Conference on Change Management* assembled contributions from top leaders and other experts on organizational transitions. In *The Manager's Pocket Guide to Creativity* (1998), he extended his work to the leadership of innovative teams and organizations.

Hiam's work on motivational leadership methods for the workplace was initially described in detail in his book *Motivating & Rewarding Employees: New and Better Ways to Inspire Your People* (1999). He extended his treatment of leadership styles and workforce motivation in chapters dedicated to these topics in *The 24 Hour MBA* (2000).

His firm has researched and developed a variety of leadership assessment, planning, and training designs, published for use by government and corporate training departments in such titles as *The Strategic Leadership Type Indicator, Profile of Leadership Opportunities,* and *Leadership Action Planning.* His studies of high-performance workplaces led to a compilation of leadership action ideas in his recent book, *Making Horses Drink* (2002). The American Management Association recently published a book based on his advanced leadership seminars, entitled *Motivational Management* (AMACOM, 2003).

Hiam has provided leadership development and training for managers at a wide variety of organizations, including AT&T, Eaton, Ford, Volvo, GM, Kellogg's, Coca Cola, Dash.com, S.C. Johnson & Sons, Young & Rubicam, Linkage, McLeod USA, Association of Independent Trust Companies, HealthEast, USDA Graduate School, and the U.S. Postal Service. He has also helped train Federal employees from the U.S. Coast Guard, the Navy, the FBI, the USDA, the U.S. Senate, and other organizations (see insightsfortraining.com for a fuller and current listing).

Hiam received his AB in anthropology from Harvard College and his MBA in strategic planning from the Haas School of Business at U.C. Berkeley. He has also lectured in MBA programs at Western New England College and American International College and was most recently on the faculty of the School of Business at U Mass Amherst. His firm maintains offices in Amherst (Mass.), Toronto, and San Francisco, and he has served on the boards of directors of the Northern California Human Resources Association and a number of nonprofits and charitable foundations.

Alex is an enthusiastic supporter of the *Woods Hole Oceanographic Institution* and encourages readers with an interest in the subject to learn more about it. He also tries to apply his interests in leadership and motivation to his volunteer work as a soccer coach, in his role as a parent of three children, and in his experiences as a sailboat captain.

FYI:

Workshops and Publications

INSIGHTS for Training & Development offers a range of leadership workshops and training materials related to this book. The Strategic Leadership program and the Motivational Management program are both closely related to the story and methods described in this book. Please call **413-549-6100** or visit **www.insightsfortraining.com** for more information or to find out about training programs, off-the-shelf training and assessment materials, custom training design, and other books on the subject of leadership.

INSIGHTS
for Training & Development